D1774852

9781584774525

WITHDRAWN
UTSA LIBRARIES

THE SYSTEM OF TAXATION IN CHINA IN THE TSING DYNASTY, 1644-1911

STUDIES IN HISTORY, ECONOMICS AND PUBLIC LAW

EDITED BY THE FACULTY OF POLITICAL SCIENCE
OF COLUMBIA UNIVERSITY

Volume LIX]   [Number 2
Whole Number 143

THE SYSTEM OF TAXATION IN CHINA IN THE TSING DYNASTY, 1644-1911

BY

SHAO-KWAN CHEN

AMS PRESS

NEW YORK

COLUMBIA UNIVERSITY
STUDIES IN THE
SOCIAL SCIENCES

143

The series was formerly known as
Studies in History, Economics and Public Law.

Reprinted with the permission of Columbia University Press
From the edition of 1914, New York
First AMS EDITION published 1970
Manufactured in the United States of America

Library of Congress Catalog Card Number: 79-120215
International Standard Book Number:
    Complete Set: 0-404-51000-0
    Number 143: 0-404-51143-0

AMS PRESS, INC.
New York, N.Y. 10003

To the

MEMORY OF MY FATHER

MR. BING-CHANG CHEN

WHO DIED IN 1913 WHEN I
WAS STUDYING IN THE
UNITED STATES

PREFACE

THE several Chinese standard works on the institutions of the *Tsing* Dynasty, 1644-1911, give us simply historical descriptions of taxation and there seems to be room for a scientific treatise, not too detailed in historical facts of similar nature or in local variations of insignificance, designed for both Occidental and Oriental readers wishing a general survey of our taxation system as it survives to-day. The present work is an attempt to generalize logically the facts connected with taxation in the *Tsing* Dynasty and to interpret their causes and effects scientifically. It includes those taxes of considerable importance which are universally imposed in all the provinces. It is not worth while to discuss those taxes which have not developed into the typical systems of the *Tsing* Dynasty either due to their insignificant yield or due to the fact that they are merely provincial special taxes which have been created during the last two decades of financial chaos, and subject only to the temporary regulations of the respective provinces. On the other hand, the discussion of the political organization is absolutely necessary to a clear conception of the system. Consequently, we have to treat the government of the *Tsing* Dynasty and its expenditures and revenues. In connection with this treatment, the same plan of generalization and interpretation is followed.

As to the sources of information, the facts have been selected chiefly from the two standard works published by the government, *viz.*, the *Institutes of the Tsing Dynasty,* and the *Amendments of the Institutes of the Tsing Dynasty.*

The facts have been chosen as carefully as possible and arranged systematically according to my plan. In the main, the work of generalization and interpretation is based upon personal knowledge and observation. In this way, it is hoped that the present work will fulfil the object of rendering service to the readers. But it must be frankly admitted that this work is by no means satisfactory from the statistical standpoint, but this is because nobody can solve the mystery of the financial conditions in all the provinces of China owing to the inefficiency of the financial control.[1]

My chief obligations in connection with this book are to Professor E. R. A. Seligman, for the sincere inspiration and the valuable supervision of the whole work, and to Mr. R. M. Haig for his valuable review of the manuscript, his numerous suggestions and his reading of the proof.

SHAO-KWAN CHEN.

COLUMBIA UNIVERSITY, MARCH 26, 1914.

[1] *Cf. infra*, pp. 106-107.

CONTENTS

CHAPTER I

The Chinese Government

CHAPTER II

Expenditures and Revenues

CHAPTER III

Taxation of Land

CHAPTER IV

Taxation of Salt

CHAPTER V

TAXATION OF COMMODITIES

CHAPTER I

The Chinese Government, 1644-1911 [1]

Forms of Government

EVEN though her great philosophers, like Confucius, Mencius and many others, advocated the theory of democracy, China, before 1911, was a monarchy. Its most important aspects may be described as follows:

(1) The Chinese government was monarchic, hereditary and unlimited. It was monarchic and unlimited, because the Emperor, representing the state as well as the government, possessed both the sovereign and the governmental powers of the land. Furthermore, the hereditary principle was maintained not only by the right of inheritance but also as a means to the end of stable government.

(2) The Chinese government was consolidated and centralized. It was not divided into three independent departments, as the legislature, the executive and the judiciary. The Emperor, in the exercise of his powers, found it necessary to create several departments to take charge of the legislation and supervision of laws and several judicial courts to administer justice. These offices, together with the Council of State, generally known as the Grand Council, constituted, as we shall see, the imperial government.

---

[1] The reorganization of government in the period 1906-1911 is not considered for three reasons. (a) It did not affect the typical system of the *Tsing* Dynasty. (b) It was an unnecessary and unsystematic reform causing a confusion of powers rather than a better distribution of powers. (c) It bore no relation to the tax systems.

Subordinate to it were the provincial governments, each with a governor [1] at its head. Owing to the fact that a highly centralized government was not suited to a state like China with vast territory and different economic conditions, numerous grants of powers had to be made to the governors in order that they might adapt the execution of the laws to local conditions. But this does not mean that the Chinese government was decentralized. First of all, the governors were subject to the will of the Emperor. Secondly, the heads of the imperial governmental departments made the laws which the governors were bound to obey, unless they disregarded certain laws with the consent of the Emperor. Thirdly, the grand councillors, being the advisers of the Emperor, were more influential than any other high officials in the imperial and provincial governments.

In conclusion, China had a monarchic, hereditary, unlimited, consolidated and centralized government. Unfortunately, the political philosophies of Confucius and many other great writers were not carried out in early times, and China did not become a democratic state until the Revolution of 1911. With the exception of the Emperor, however, the whole government rested upon a popular basis, because the candidates for lower offices were chosen by competitive examinations held in the national and provincial capitals, while the vacancies of higher offices were filled by those selected among the lower officials. It is true that only a minority of the subjects participated in the actual work of government. But every male subject had equal chance to pass the examinations in order to be admitted to the government. In case of failure in any one examination, he might take a series of examinations during his life. Al-

---

[1] In this book, I identify the governor-general with the governor. For the reason of this, *cf. infra*, pp. 23-24.

though the ideal government is one in which every member of the state has a share, a government such as the one which existed, in which every member might have a share, is far from undesirable.

The Emperor

As China was a monarchic state, the Emperor enjoyed the sovereign power. His powers were neither enumerated nor residual. He might be deprived of power only by a successful revolution. As long as he was in power, the governmental machinery was created and preserved by him, and all the officials thereof were responsible only to him. His orders were the laws of the country. By the word " order " is meant not merely his personal orders but also all the laws, drafted by his ministers with or without amendments by him, and promulgated by him in the form of an imperial order. In foreign relations, he represented the country. Treaties and other agreements were promulgated by imperial orders as a part of the law of the land. Of course, he also had power to declare both offensive and defensive wars.

The Council of State

(1) The Inner Cabinet. The Inner Cabinet (*Nai Ko*) was the old Council of State. It had two Chinese and two Manchu ministers appointed by the Emperor through the nomination of the Inner Cabinet itself. In addition, there were two or four associate ministers, of which one-half were Chinese and the other half Manchus. They were selected from the heads of departments by the Emperor himself. Under these ministers there were different classes of secretaries. Their most important functions were:

(a) The discussion of state affairs.

(b) The promulgation of imperial orders.

(c) The conduct of great ceremonials attended by the Emperor.

The Inner Cabinet lasted until the end of the *Tsing* Dynasty. But its great powers had been gradually transferred to the Military Council.

(2) The Military Council. The Military Council (*Tsuen Tse Chu*), known to the Western people as the Grand Council, was created by Emperor Yung Tsing, 1723-1735, primarily for the discussion of military affairs. It was not an established office but simply a body of advisers of the Emperor. Its members were chosen from the ministers of the Inner Cabinet and the heads of different departments, and called the Ministers of Military Affairs or Grand Councillors. The number was not fixed, varying from four to six. Being the advisers of the Emperor, they gradually encroached upon the power of the Inner Cabinet with respect to the civil affairs. They had a certain number of secretaries. Their chief powers and duties were as follows:

(a) The issue of decrees to announce the Emperor's acts, to approve or veto a memorial, to order an approved memorial to be adopted in the provinces and to order a governor's memorial to be considered by a department.

(b) The issue of orders to give instructions to the Imperial Ministers in the dependencies and to the governors in the provinces.

(c) The discussion of state affairs.

(d) The trial of the most important judicial cases whenever ordered by the Emperor.

(e) The investigation of military and financial affairs in time of war.

(f) The nomination of cabinet ministers, heads of departments, governors, heads of provincial departments, certain circuit governors, certain prefects, generals, lieutenant-generals, commissioners of examinations and superintendents of customs.

The Department of Foreign Affairs

Organization and functions. The Department of Foreign Affairs was created in 1861 under the name *Tsung Li Yâmen*. It was controlled by a number of princes, ministers and adjunct ministers. The various classes of departmental heads, whose number was not fixed, were selected by the Emperor himself, the princes from the various classes of princes, the ministers from the ministers of the Military Council (the Council of State),[1] the adjunct ministers from the ministers of the Inner Cabinet (the old Council of State)[2] and the heads of the other departments. Their functions were to make all kinds of treaties and agreements involving the tariff, the regulation of international commerce, the questions of territories, the settlement of relations between the non-Christians and Christians and other kinds of intercourse. These functions were distributed among a general committee and five special committees which were made up by a certain number of Chinese and Manchu secretaries.

The Departments of Internal Affairs

Organization and functions. Among the departments which are not worthy of consideration so far as actual government is concerned, six were well developed, namely, the civil-service, financial, ceremonial, military, judicial and public works departments. All the different matters requiring attention from the government would fall under one of these six departments. Each department had two presidents, one being Chinese and the other Manchus, and four vice-presidents, two being Chinese and the other two Manchus. It was found necessary to make a further division of work, and thus a certain number of bureaus were estab-

---

[1] *Cf. supra*, p. 14.   [2] *Cf. supra*, p. 13.

lished in each department.   The distribution of business among the bureaus was made in accordance with its nature. But this method was not always followed, because the quantity of certain matters was too great to be transacted by a single bureau.   In that case the work was divided according to geographical lines as well as according to the nature of the function.   In other words, a function was generally discharged by several bureaus.   Each bureau had three classes of secretaries, and each class consisted of a certain number of Chinese, Mongolians and Manchus.

The Department of Finance (Hu-Pu)

Among the six departments of internal affairs as mentioned above, the Department of Finance should be described more fully, because the administration of finance was one of the most important functions of the Chinese government.   It framed and supervised the laws concerning territory and population.   It had power to divide the country into administrative divisions,[1] *viz.*, provinces, prefectures and districts; to classify the population according to the permanent occupation and home; to survey the land of the country; to equalize the burden of taxation and service; to appropriate the ordinary expenditures of the government; and to adjust the amount of reserved grain.   It had the following bureaus:

(A) The Bureau of *Kiang-nan*[2] audited the accounts of the land tax of *Kiang-nan* Provinces and the accounts of the government silk factories in the City of *Nan-king* and the City of *Soo-chow* in *Kiang-su* Province; and prepared the annual reports concerning the amount of the balance

---

[1] *Cf. infra*, pp. 22-23.

[2] *Kiang-nan* is the collective name of the two provinces, *Kiang-su* and *An-hwei*.

charge[1] of the land tax in certain provinces, and the deferred payment of the land tax in all the provinces.

(B) The Bureau of *Che-kiang* audited the accounts of the land tax of *Che-kiang* Province and the accounts of the government silk factory in the City of *Hang-chow* in *Che-kiang* Province; and prepared the annual reports concerning the number of population and the quantity of grain produced in all the provinces.

(C) The Bureau of *Kiang-si* audited the accounts of the land tax of *Kiang-si* Province; and prepared the reports of the inter-provincial support of military expenses.

(D) The Bureau of *Fu-kien* audited (a) the accounts of duties on commodities carried in native vessels to *Tien-tsin, Chi-li* Province; (b) the accounts of the land tax of *Fu-kien* and *Chi-li* Provinces; and (c) the accounts of certain unprescribed expenses drawn from the treasury of the Department of Finance.

(E) The Bureau of *Hu-kwang*[2] audited (a) the accounts of the land tax of *Hu-kwang* Provinces; (b) the accounts of regular customs in *Hu-peh* Province; and (c) the accounts of local supplementary taxes on land, commodities (*i. e.*, regular customs duties), salt and tea in all the provinces.

(F) The Bureau of *Shan-tung* had the following duties:

(a) The auditing of the accounts of the land tax of *Shang-tung, Feng-tien, Ki-rin* and *Hei-lung-kiang* Provinces.

(b) The payment of bonus to the " Eight Banners "[3] military officers.

[1] This is charged for the loss due to inaccurate weighing.

[2] *Hu-kwang* is the collective name of the two provinces, *Hu-peh* and *Hu-nan*.

[3] The Tartar soldiers are divided into eight corps, each having a colored banner, *viz.*, pure yellow, mixed yellow, pure white, mixed white, pure red, mixed red, pure blue and mixed blue. The Chinese force has the green banner.

(c) The control of salt and ginseng monopolies.

(G) The Bureau of *Shan-si* audited the accounts of the land tax of *Shan-si* Province.

(H) The Bureau of *Ho-nan* audited the accounts of the land tax of *Ho-nan* Province, and the military expenses of the City of Sahara in Mongolia; investigated any report designated by the Emperor; and urged the revision of provincial reports on any sort of outlay not accepted by the Department of Finance.

(I) The Bureau of *Shen-si* discharged three functions, namely,

(a) The auditing of the accounts of the land tax of *Shen-si, Kan-su* and Chinese Turkestan Provinces.

(b) The control of the tea monopoly.

(c) The disbursement of the expenditures of the imperial government.

(J)   The Bureau of *Sze-chuen,* in addition to its other minor duties, performed the following two functions:

(a) The auditing of the accounts of the land tax and regular custom revenues of *Sze-chuen* Province.

(b) The collection of reports on the condition of harvest in all the provinces.

(K) The Bureau of *Kwang-tung* audited the accounts of the land tax of *Kwang-tung* Province.

(L) The Bureau of *Kwang-si* was entrusted with the following important business:

(a) The auditing of the accounts of the land tax and regular customs duties of *Kwang-si* Province.

(b) The regulation of mining.

(c) The coinage.

(M) The Bureau of *Yun-nan* had charge of the following affairs:

(a) The auditing of the accounts of the land tax of *Yun-nan* Province.

(b) The investigation of the report on the collection of mining royalty in *Yun-nan* Province.

(c) The care of matters concerning the transportation of grain from certain provinces to Peking.

(N) The Bureau of *Kwei-chow* audited the accounts of the land tax of *Kwei-chow* Province, and supervised the administration of both the regular and maritime customs throughout the country.

In addition to the above fourteen bureaus there were the following organizations:

(A) Three treasuries, *viz.*, money, satin and sundry articles, under the control of four ministers appointed on the nomination of the department.

(B) Four mints in Peking under the control of two vice-presidents of the department.

(C) Thirteen granaries in Peking and *Peh-tung-chow* [1] under the control of two high officials having the rank of a vice-president of a department.

(D) The Committee of Appropriation.[2]

(E) The Committee of Cash Payment of the "Eight Banners" Soldiers.

General Position and Powers of Heads of Departments

The heads of every department were appointed and removed by the Emperor with or without the advice of the Council of State. They assumed joint responsibility to the Emperor only. They, however, might be impeached by any high official or censor who had power to present memorials to the Throne. But an impeachment did not necessarily cause the removal of a departmental head, because the Emperor might not approve the impeachment. Therefore, any head of a department remained in service

---

[1] *Peh-tung-chow* is a river port near Peking.

[2] *Cf. infra*, p. 34.

until removed for one of the following causes, *viz.*, promotion, change, degradation or dismissal of office, death of parents, absence, or retirement. There follows a summary of the general powers of the heads of departments.

(1) The participation in the conference on important matters ordered to be discussed by the nine departments.[1]

(2) The making and amendment of laws subject to the approval of the Emperor.

(3) The supervision in the execution of laws. This means that the heads of departments had power to approve or disapprove the provincial reports concerning the exercise of functions. But they had no right to direct the governors how to execute the laws because they did not know the local conditions.

(4) The nomination of certain subordinate officials, not nominated by the Department of Civil Service.

(5) The removal of subordinate officials by impeachment through memorials presented to the Throne. Such impeachments were usually accepted by the Emperor.

(6) The direction and supervision of the subordinate officials.

The Censorate

(1) Organization. The Censorate (*Tu-Tsar Yuen*) had at its head two chief censors (a Chinese and a Manchus) and four associate censors (two Chinese and two Manchus) who were appointed by the Emperor. Under them there were six groups of censors adopting the names of the six departments, *viz.*, civil, financial, ceremonial, military, judicial and public works, and fifteen groups of censors taking

---

[1] The nine departments include the six departments mentioned above, *viz.*, the civil, financial, ceremonial, military, judicial and public works departments, and in addition the Censorate, the High Court and the Department for the Transmission of Memorials.

the names of the different provinces. Each group of censors was composed of two Chinese and two Manchus. They were appointed among the candidates of censors who had been previously selected from the secretaries of various departments.

(2) Powers of the censors. The general duty of the chief censors and associate censors was to look after the faithful execution of the laws of the country and to prevent violation of law or neglect by any official, either imperial or provincial. They were vested with freedom of speech. The departmental censors and provincial censors were supposed to assist the chief censors and associate censors in the exercise of the general power of the Censorate. But they also had the right to communicate freely with the Emperor by means of memorials. When any censor did not satisfy the Emperor, he was ordered to return to his previous department without punishment.

The Less Important Departments

Besides the foregoing branches there were many other offices of which only the following need be mentioned:

(1) The Department of Dependencies' Affairs (*Li Fan Yuen*).

(2) The Department of the Imperial Clan's Affairs (*Tsung Yin Fu*).

(3) The Department of Palace Affairs (*Nui Wu Feu*).

(4) The Department of Astronomy (*Tsin Tien Tsan*).

(5) The Department of Imperial Doctors (*Tai Yi Yuen*).

(6) The Department of Literary Men (*Han Lin Yuen*).

(7) The Department of Heir Tutors (*Tsien Shi Feu*).

(8) The Department of Imperial Worship Ceremonies (*Tai Shiang Tsi*).

(9) The Department of Horse-Breeding (*Tai Pu Tsi*).

(10) The Department of Imperial Feasts (*Kwang Lu Tsi*).

(11) The Department of Palace Ceremonies (*Heng Lu Tsi*).

(12) The High Court (*Ta Li Tsi*).

Territorial Divisions of Government

Excluding Mongolia and Tibet, China was divided into twenty-two provinces (*Sheng*). In some cases, a province was governed by a governor-general (*Tsung Tu*), such as *Chi-li* and *Sze-chuen*. In other cases a province had a governor (*Shün Fu*), for example, *Shan-tung, Shan-si,* and *Ho-nan*. In general, a more important province was under the immediate jurisdiction of a governor-general, while a less important province was governed by a governor with the nominal supervision of a governor-general. Under the governor-general or governor were the heads of the Executive Department (*Bu Tseng Shi*), and the Judicial Department (*An Tsar Shi*) and a number of circuit governors (*Tao Tai*). Each province was composed of a number of prefectures (*Fu*) and direct districts (*Chi Li Chow* or *Chi Li Ting*),[1] so-called because they were under the direct control of the Executive Department like the prefectures. The ruler of a prefecture was called a prefect (*Tsi Fu*), and that of a direct district, a superior magistrate (*Chi Li Chow Tsi Chow* or *Chi Li Ting Tung Tsi*),[2] and he was charged with the functions of a magistrate and the powers of a prefect. The lowest but most important units of administration were the districts (*Shien*),[3] several of which made up a prefecture or a direct district. The ad-

---

[1] Certain *Chi Li Ting* were not composed of a number of subordinate districts as all the *Chi Li Chow* were.

[2] Certain *Chi Li Ting Tung Tsi* had not the powers of a prefect as all the *Chi Li Chow Tsi Chow* had. See note 1.

[3] Some districts were called in Chinese *Ting* or *Chow*.

ministrator of a district was called a magistrate (*Tsi Shien*).[1]   All the above officials were known as the sealholders (*Tseng Yin Kwan*), *i. e.*, the chief officers or responsible officers.   Their respective subordinates were regarded merely as assistant officers, and could not act without instructions.

Provincial Administration

(1) The governor-general or governor.. The governorgeneral or governor was appointed by the Emperor.   The governor-general also had the titles of the Chief Censor of the Censorate and the President of the Department of Military Service; and the governor, the titles of the Associate Censor of the Censorate and the Vice-President of the Department of Military Service. Both of them remained in service unless prevented by promotion, change, degradation or dismissal of office, retirement, death of parents or absence. The governor-general was different from the governor inasmuch as that the former had the nominal power of supervision over the government in the latter's sphere of authority, besides the virtual powers of direction and supervision over the administration of his own immediate jurisdiction. Practically, however, each province had only one head, either a governor-general or a governor. The powers of the governor-general or governor may be fully stated as follows:

(A) The nomination of certain circuit governors, prefects, magistrates and military officers lower than the lieutenant-generals.

(B) The removal, by means of impeachment, of any civil or military official appointed through the Council of State, the Department of Civil Service and the Department of Military Service as well as through his own nomination.

---

[1] Some magistrates were called in Chinese *Tung Tsi* (the administrator of a *Ting*) or *Tsi Chow* (the administrator of a *Chow*).

(C) Such direction and supervision of the actions of all his subordinates as seemed desirable.

(D) The furnishing of such supplementary ordinances as might be necessary to the execution of law, subject to the approval of the Emperor.

(E) Remonstrances to laws or appointments. If the Emperor accepted the objection, the laws or appointments were ordered to be amended or changed by the departments. Otherwise the governor had to accept them.

(F) The initiation of laws which were generally ordered to be discussed by the departments.

(G) The execution of laws.

(H) The administration of justice.

(I) The command of the Chinese forces within the jurisdiction. Armed with these powers, the governor-general or governor proceeded to discharge his executive and judicial functions through the Executive Department and the Judicial Department.

(2) The Executive Department and the Judicial Department. The tenure and term of office of the head of each department were the same as those of the governor. Each head of department had the right to direct and supervise the actions of all his subordinates. It was through the division of functions according to their character that these two departments were distinguished from each other. In other words, the Executive Department discharged the executive functions, of which the most important is the financial; and the Judicial Department had to try and to determine the cases of appeals and to give the final decisions of cases involving murder or robbery, removed from the districts.

(3) The circuit governor was appointed on the nomination of the governor or the Department of Civil Service, except in a very few cases when the Emperor made the appointment. After the expiration of a term of six, seven

or eight years[1] the circuit governor was usually promoted; otherwise he remained in service until he encountered one of the following conditions: change, degradation, removal from office, retirement, death of parents or absence. He was charged with the general duty of preserving public order within his circuit composed of a number of prefectures and direct districts. In fulfilling his duty, he acted as a connecting link between the civil officials and the military officers. In other words, he was the man to judge when it was necessary to use arms for the suppression of riots, the execution of laws and the administration of justice. He had power to direct and supervise the prefects and magistrates and to demand the help of the Chinese forces in his circuit. For governmental purposes he resided in the most important city in his circuit.

Local Administration

(1) The prefect. The tenure and term of office of the ruler of a prefecture were similar to those of the circuit governor. He had no territory and population under his own immediate government.[2] His powers were to try and to determine the cases of appeals, to review the cases originally decided by the magistrates and to direct and supervise the actions of all his subordinates.

(2) The superior magistrate. Each direct district was divided into several parts, one of which was under the immediate government of the superior magistrate himself, while the other parts, constituting the subordinate districts, were governed by a corresponding number of magistrates under his supervision. It was noticed that the tenure of

---

[1] The duration of term was different in different provinces.

[2] The prefects of a few prefectures had immediate jurisdictions. In those cases the powers and duties of the prefects were like those of the superior magistrates.

office and functions of the superior magistrate were like those of a magistrate, the term of office being six, seven or eight years. The former was distinguished from the latter only by the possession of the powers of a prefect.

NUMBER OF LOCAL ADMINISTRATIVE DISTRICTS IN THE DIFFERENT PROVINCES

Province [1]	Districts	Direct Districts	Total
Chi-li	144	11	155
Feng-tien	21	3	24
Ki-rin	7	2	9
Hei-lung-kiang		2	2
Shan-tung	105	2	107
Shan-si	98	10	108
Ho-nan	103	4	107
Kiang-su	67	4	71
An-hwei	55	5	60
Kiang-si	78	1	79
Fu-kien	64	2	66
Che-kiang	78	1	79
Hu-peh	67	1	68
Hu-nan	67	9	76
Shen-si	85	5	90
Kan-su	59	7	66
Turkestan	11	15	26
Sze-chuen	131	12	143
Kwang-tung	85	10	95
Kwang-si	66	5	71
Yun-nan	75	8	83
Kwei-chow	57	15	72
Total	1523	134	1657

[1] The figures of *Chi-li, Feng-tien, Ki-rin, Kwang-si* and *Kwei-chow* include those administrative units under the immediate administration of the prefects themselves. These units were practically direct districts, and the prefects had exactly the same powers and duties of superior magistrates. Owing to thin population and restriction of cultivation, Manchuria (*Feng-tien, Ki-rin, Hei-lung-kiang*) and Turkestan had not been organized as provinces until in late years, Turkestan in 1884 and Manchuria in 1906. In 1902 nine districts were added to the original number in Turkestan; in the period 1906-1907 nine districts, in *Ki-rin*; and in the period 1904-1908 thirty-five districts, in *Hei-lung-kiang*.

(3) The magistrate. The ruler of a subordinate district of a prefecture or a direct district was called the magistrate. The magistrates of certain districts were appointed on the nomination of the governor, while in other districts they were selected by the Department of Civil Service. After the expiration of a term of ten years the magistrate was usually promoted; otherwise he remained in service as long as one of the following conditions did not arise: change, degradation or dismissal from office, retirement, death of parents or absence. Under the direction and supervision of his superior officials, he discharged the following functions:

(A) The execution of all the administrative laws.

(B) The trial and decision of original cases. But the decisions involving the penalty of banishment for a limited time were subject to the approval of the prefect or superior magistrate; and the cases of murder or robbery were entitled to a second trial by the prefect or superior magistrate and to the final decision of the head of the Judicial Department.

Original cases involving robbery or murder committed in the immediate jurisdiction of a prefect or superior magistrate and decided by him, must be approved or retried by the circuit governor.

General Features of Government

In conclusion, we may summarize the important features of the Chinese Government as follows:

(1) The authority of general powers. As the Emperor was the sovereign of the state, he was the final interpreter of the laws of the land. He settled the conflicts of opinions among his ministers whether they were the heads of departments, governors or others, because they were dependent for tenure upon him. In order to assist him in the exercise of his powers he had the Council of State. In any case which involved the councillors, he was obliged to decide without the advice of any other person.

(2) The legislative powers. Instead of vesting the legislative powers in a single organization known as the legislature, the Emperor distributed them among several departments according to the nature of their functions. The seven chief departments at Peking were really legislative departments although they were not shut out from all participation in the work of administration, *e. g.*, foreign relations, appropriations of revenue, conduct of public ceremonials and examinations *etc*. In the main these departments were concerned with making and interpreting laws. This may be illustrated step by step. In the first place, treaties concluded by the Department of Foreign Affairs were a part of the laws. In the second place, the nominations by the Department of Civil Service and the Department of Military Service for official appointments and removals was merely an interpretation of the civil and military service laws made by the same. In the third place, the executive functions of the Department of Finance, the Department of Military Service and the Department of Public Works were mainly connected with the control of finance. In the fourth place, the Department of Public Ceremonials and the Department of Military Service merely regulated the matters of public examinations of civil and military services, because the examinations were actually conducted by the Imperial Examiners, appointed by the Emperor.

(3) The executive powers. The executive powers were distributed not according to functions but according to territories. Therefore, the provincial governments together form the executive branch of the central government. In each province, the governor was the chief executive. The detailed work of administration was performed by the Executive Department, while the general powers of direction and supervision were delegated to the circuit governors. But the governor was not deprived of all participation in

the work of legislation and in the administration of justice, because he had not only the power to initiate laws, to object to them and to issue orders but he had also the power to control the Judicial Department of his province.

(4) Participation of the localities in administration. The local officials known as the prefects, the superior magistrates and the magistrates were regarded simply as agents of the central government. All the duties to be performed by the localities were fixed by the legislative branch of the central government (the chief department at Peking). Still there was a realm of action in which the local authorities possessed large discretion, and they look for their authority to the executive branch of the central government (the provincial governments). Thus it is evident that the local authorities were subject to both the legislative and administrative control.

(5) Subordination of the judicial powers to the other authorities. The judicial powers, on the one hand, were subordinated to the executive, because they were exercised by the Judicial Department and the local authorities, subject to the supervision of the governor. On the other hand, they were subject to the legislature, because the Department of Judicial Affairs exerted the greatest influence over all judicial cases.

(6) The control over the government. While the heads of departments at Peking and the governors in the provinces controlled the actions of their respective subordinate officials, their actions were in turn controlled by the Emperor himself. Besides this, there were five other methods of control. First, the Censorate might hear complaint by any one person against any other person, no matter whether the parties involved were officials or not, and report the case to the Emperor. Secondly, any censor might impeach any official. Thirdly, any minister might impeach any other

minister.   Fourthly, the Department of Civil Service might impeach any civil official according to the civil service laws. Fifthly, the Department of Military Service might impeach any military officer in accordance with the military service laws.   Having received the case or impeachment, the Emperor referred it to the proper authority, or appointed one or more ministers to investigate the matter in detail.

(7) An attempt to secure efficient administration in the provinces.   The Department of Civil Service had power to consider the right of changing domicile.[1]   Such questions arose when an official applied for naturalization in his residential province, which was not his ancestral province, or when he sought to reclaim his standing in his ancestral province after he had once become naturalized in his residential province.[2]   These questions were numerous, because the law forbade a man to be an official of his native province.   Undoubtedly this legal limitation had several advantages from the point of view of efficiency of administration in the provinces.   First, when an official was a stranger in a community, the community, having no intimate relation with him, could exert less influence over his actions.   Secondly, the government was free to choose proper men to fill the official posts from the people of all the provinces except one, without incurring the danger of bad feelings among the local communities.   Finally, the officials assumed responsibility to the government rather than to the different communities under their respective jurisdiction, if they desired to maintain their positions.

---

[1] In China the domicile was determined by the domicile of one's ancestors rather than by one's birthplace.

[2] The qualifications of admission were the possession of certain kinds of real property, such as a house or a piece of land, and twenty years of residence by his grand-parents or parents.

CHAPTER II

Expenditures and Revenues

Classification of Expenditures

From a review of the government functions during the *Tsing* Dynasty, it appears that the public expenditures of China may be classified as follows:

(1) Expenditures for military purposes.
   (A) Regular pay of officers and men.
   (B) Additional pay of officers.
(2) Expenditures for civil administration.
   (A) Salaries of civil officials.
   (B) Additional allowances of civil officials.
(3) Expenditures for the Emperor's family.
   (A) Imperial tombs' furnishing.
   (B) New Year expenses of the Emperor's family.
   (C) Silk manufactures for the Emperor's use and public use.
(4) Expenditures for communication.
(5) Expenditures for the conservation of rivers and ponds.
(6) Expenditures for social purposes.
   (A) Public worship.
   (B) Public gifts and charities.
   (C) Public schools and scholarships.
   (D) Public examinations for the selection of competent men as candidates for public offices.
(7) Expenditures for miscellaneous purposes.

Comparative Importance of Expenditures

Among all classes of expenditures, the military expenditures stood in the first rank, because the existence of a state depends especially on peace. Without an army of sufficient strength, it is impossible to protect the weak members of a society against the encroachment of the strong, and to save the country from the foreign conquest. Next came the expenditures of civil administration which is necessary for the maintenance of internal order in a civil society. The two items in the following table of expenditures, styled the additional allowances of civil and military officials, are due to the fact that the regular salaries did not suffice to meet the higher standard of living. Thirdly, the Emperor was a great consumer of public revenues. The three items constituting the expenditures of the Emperor's family are by no means exhaustive. They merely represent those sums paid out of the treasury of the Department of Finance and of the provincial treasuries. For two reasons, it is impossible to discover the amount of revenues wasted by the Emperor. The Department of Palace Affairs, which was charged with the administration of the imperial finances, was not subject to the supervision of the Department of Finance. Moreover, a great many departments of civil administration were established primarily for the Emperor and their expenses cannot be isolated. In the fourth place, the postal stations were established primarily for military and other government services instead of for industrial, fiscal or other purposes. The object of the expenditures for the conservation of rivers and ponds was to protect agricultural land against flood or draught. Next follow the expenditures for social purposes which were composed of four elements.

(a) Public worship.

(b) Public gifts and charities, which included the purchase of boards bearing signs for identifying obedient sons, unmarried widows, persons over one hundred years old, the gifts of five hundred *sinc* rice and ten rolls of cloth to any woman giving birth to three sons at the same day, the expenses connected with care of widows, widowers, fatherless or motherless children, criminals and the defective and helpless classes.

(c) Public schools and scholarships for the support of poor students in the district schools.

(d) Public examinations for the selection of competent men as candidates for public offices.[1]

According to the order of importance, the Department of Finance made the permanent appropriations for various functions. In addition there were extraordinary, uncertain or insignificant outlays.

THE STATUS OF THE PERMANENT APPROPRIATIONS DURING THE NINE-
TEENTH CENTURY

Regular Pay of Military Officers and Men	14,862,929[2]
Additional Pay of Military Officers	1,398,755
Sundry Expenses in the Army	274,523
Regular Pay of Chinese and Manchu Troops in Peking	5,348,556
Regular Salaries of Civil Officials	1,908,086
Additional Allowance of Civil Officials	2,937,369
Salaries of Civil and Military Officials [3] in Peking	196,988
Imperial Tomb's Furnishing	106,861
New Year Expenses of the Imperial Family Paid in Peking	180,000
Silk Manufactures	107,833
Postal Stations	2,147,961
Conservation of Rivers and Ponds	1,618,081
Public Worship	210,615
Public Gifts and Charities	217,420
Public Schools and Scholarships	197,749
Miscellaneous Expenses	415,957
Total	32,129,683

[1] *Cf.* Y. S. Ho, *Chinese Education from the Western Viewpoint* (New York, 1913), pp. 34-41.

[2] The figures are in *taels*.   [3] Manchus are not included.

Sources of Public Revenues

In modern countries the revenues expended for public purposes are often derived from a variety of sources. In consequence of economic conditions, China, up to the late years, was content with only one form of revenue, namely, taxation.

The Department of Finance classified the sources of revenues into five items, namely, land taxes (*Fu*); rents (*Tsoo*); royalties (*Kau*); duties (*Shui*); and tributes (*Kung*).[1] For the convenience of consideration, it seems better to adopt the following classification:

(1) Taxation of agricultural lands including taxes and rents.

(2) Taxation of salt (royalties).

(3) Taxation of commodities (duties), including regular customs duties and *li-kin* duties.

Appropriations

Having learned in the preceding sections the different classes of functions with their amounts of appropriated revenues and the various sources of revenues, it is now possible to discuss the seasonal appropriations of revenues made by the Committee of Appropriation in the Department of Finance. The committee was authorized by the heads of the department to appropriate revenues for military purposes in the winter, and for all other purposes during the spring and autumn upon the basis of the provincial reports of the amount of collected revenues. These appropriations were necessary for two reasons. First, there were various uncertain elements of ordinary expenditures which could not be accurately estimated and provided for beforehand in

---

[1] Tributes and other insignificant sources of royalties and duties are not worth consideration.

the permanent appropriations.[1] In the second place, the balance of outlays and incomes in the different provinces might be favorable or unfavorable. In addition to the seasonal appropriations, which were general in character, there were special appropriations to meet the extraordinary expenditures whenever they occurred. Appropriations were made according to functions and provinces, because practically all district expenditures which can be embodied in the permanent appropriations were permitted to be deducted from the land tax.

The collection of revenues provided to meet the appropriations was controlled partly by central and partly by local officials. First, the land tax which is levied in every province was divided into two parts. One part was deducted by the magistrate[2] for the district expenditures and was called the reserved fund, while the other part which was required to be sent to the Executive Department[3] in the provincial capital was known as the transporting fund. All other sources of revenues, such as salt royalties, maritime customs duties and regular customs duties were national in character and were administered by special officers under the supervision of the governor. These revenues together with the transporting fund of the land tax constituted the available resources for meeting both national and provincial appropriations. As soon as the appropriations had been approved by the Emperor, those provinces whose collected revenues exceeded their expenditures were required to transport their surplus revenues to Peking or to provinces in less fortunate circumstances. With the development of banking, the governors often bought bills of exchange from the prominent Chinese bankers.

---

[1] *Cf. supra*, p. 33.   [2] *Cf. infra*, pp. 64-65.
[3] *Cf. supra*, p. 24.

THE AMOUNT OF THE TRANSPORTING FUND AND THE RESERVED FUND IN
THE SEVERAL PROVINCES AS DETERMINED BY LAW

Province	The transporting fund in *taels* of silver		The reserved fund in *taels* of silver	
	Revenue from the regular tax	Revenue from the compensatory tax	Revenue from the regular tax	Revenue from the compensatory tax
Chi-li	1,708,521.486	211,856.256	672,622.111	
Feng-tien.	20,318.646	....	9,148.082	
Ki-rin	31,956.780	3,293.195	144.136	
Shan-tung	2,772,630.023	228,638.666	328,171.084	45,941.962
Shan-si [1]	2,645,503.655	272,846.752	312,540.853	86,200.748
Ho-nan [1] .	2,747,240.229	244,109.554	232,944.854	36,272.329
Kiang-su .	2,231,264.000	113,231.000	291,025.478	24,114.852
An-hwei	1,220,310.000	113,998.200	250,419.000	55,370.000
Kiang-si [1] .	1,781,607.770	86,651.970	208,547.445	
Fu-kien	1,037,992.952	13,379.707	198,762.640	4,864.483
Che-kiang	2,121,750.774	83,584.128	239,796.926	10,731.109
Hu-peh	961,768.653	71,262.860	98,403.313	10,922.769
Hu-nan	936,647.098	74,935.740	94,975.866	9,497.586
Shen-si.	1,341,361.752	66,451.728	278,122.936	170,760.000
Kan-su.	214,494.580	10,535.940	71,441.899	29,902.163
Sze-chuen	541,501.823	44,696.557	100,106.861	54,900.000
Kwang-tung [1] .	864,211.117	126,259.512	161,075.170	
Kwang-si [1]	330,845.518	12,153.603	91,207.457	
Yun-nan .	147,000.033	47,641.914	46,771,297	32,684.796
Kwei-chow .	65,864.800	5,044.100	28,030.200	14,440.751
Total	23,722,791.689	1,830,576.382	3,715,157.608	586,603.548

Transportation of Produce

(1) The necessity of produce to the Peking Government.
As we know, the land tax was paid both in money and in
produce, *viz.*, rice, wheat, beans *etc.* Whether the money

---

[1] These five provinces had an additional sum of the reserved
fund for the leap month whenever it occurred *i. e.*, *Shan-si* had
12533.366 *taels* of the regular tax and .944 *tael* of the compensatory tax; *Ho-nan*, 15828.521 *taels* of the regular tax and .038
tael of the compensatory tax; *Kiang-si*, 7446.035 *taels* of the regular
tax; *Kwang-tung*, 10493.378 *taels* of the regular tax; and *Kwang-si*,
5958.607 *taels* of the regular tax. These figures are found in *The
Amendments of the Institutes of the Tsing Dynasty*, ch. clxix-clxx.

revenues from the land tax of each province should be de-
posited in the provincial treasury, or transported to Peking
or elsewhere was determined by the appropriations of the
Department of Finance.   On the other hand, the office-
holders and troops in the different provinces received a part
of their pay out of the collected produce of their respective
provinces, while those in Peking were entitled to get their
respective partial payment in produce from certain great
producing provinces.   Thus *Shan-tung, Ho-nan, Kiang-su,
An-hwei, Kiang-si, Hu-peh, Hu-nan* and *Che-kiang* were
required to send a part of the collected produce to Peking.[1]
The quantity to be supplied by each province was legally prescribed, and no deduction or commutation to money was
permitted, unless upon extraordinary occasions, such as a
bad harvest or a rebellion.   An extra charge was demanded
for the loss in weighing, shipping or storage.

(2) Transportation and storage.   In autumn of the year
the magistrates collected the required quantity of rice and
delivered it to the transporters in the respective harbors.
This had to be done within a fixed period (within the winter
in *Shan-tung;* from the beginning of the twelfth month to
the end of the second month of the following year in the
provinces of the *Yang-tze* River; during the entire first
month and half of the second in South *Kiang-su* and *Che-
kiang*).   In those districts which were remote from the harbors, or did not produce the anticipated quantity of rice,
the required quantity of rice was paid in silver according
to a fixed rate of exchange, or according to the market
price of the collecting month.   The magistrates bought
rice in the districts surrounding the harbors or transferred the silver to the Department of Finance through
the Executive Department.   The available rice might

---

[1] The produce was also used for other purposes than the support of
public servants.

be transported by way of the Grain Canal, or Grand Canal as it is usually called by the foreigners, or by sea. Formerly, the public rice junks [1] sailing along the canal, started for *Peh-tung-chow,* the river port of Peking, in or before the second month of the year. In 1802 the rice of *Soo-chow, Sung-kiang,* and *Tai-chong* (*Kiang-su* Province) was allowed to be transported by sea via Shanghai. In 1825 Emperor Tao Kwang proposed that sea transportation be universally adopted. In 1852, the rice paid by the southern part of *Kiang-su* and *Che-Kiang* began to be transported by sea, because the public rice junks were so crowded on the canal that many junks could not arrive at *Peh-tung-chow* before the freezing of the *Peh-ho* River in the winter. From 1853 to 1864, the rice was mostly paid in money due to the *Tai-ping* Rebellion of 1850-1864, and the public junks disappeared. In 1865, the canal transportation of rice paid by the provinces north of the *Yang-tze* River was renewed and private junks were hired to displace the public rice junks. Vessels carrying South *Kiang-su* and *Che-kiang* rice continued to leave Shanghai for Tientsin by sea in the second month of the year. In 1873, the sailing vessels were replaced by the steamships of the China Merchant's Steam Navigation Company in Shanghai, while the other southern provinces sometimes sent a part of their rice by sea in the following years.

The transportation was accomplished through the aid of one transporter-in-chief,[2] four provincial transporters [3] and many military officers and men. The civil and military

[1] The number of junks in 1812 was 6242. Each junk had the privilege of carrying goods equal in value to twenty per cent of the rice free of customs duties.

[2] This official was equal in rank to a governor.

[3] These officials were equal in rank to the circuit governors. They were the heads of the grain departments in North *Kiang-su* (including *An-hwei*), South *Kiang-su, Che-kiang* and *Shan-tung.*

transporters with their soldiers went to *Peh-tung-chow* and delivered the rice of their provinces to the granary keeper-in-chief. Then the rice and other produce were kept either in the granaries in Peking and *Peh-tung-chow* at the disposal of the Peking Government or in the granaries in *Tsi-chow* and *Yi-chow* for the garrisons of the imperial tombs. For the services of collection, transportation and storage, various kinds of fees were demanded for the collectors, transporters and keepers.

After 1901, the legal quantity of produce had been commuted to money in order to save the extravagant cost of

THE QUANTITY OF RICE REQUIRED TO BE TRANSPORTED TO PEKING

Province	Rice due to the Peking Granary	Rice due to the *Peh-tung-chow* Granary	Rice due to both granaries
Shan-tung	28,000,000 *sinc*	9,560,000 *sinc*	37,560,000 *sinc*
Ho-nan	27,000,000 "	11,000,000 "	38,000,000 "
Kiang-su	111,300,000 "	9,395,000 "	120,695,000 "
An-hwei	38,700,000 "	20,045,000 "	58,745,000 "
Kiang-si	40,000,000 "	17,000,000 "	57,000,000 "
Che-Kiang ...	60,000,000 "	3,000,000 "	63,000,000 "
Hu-peh	12,294,271- "		12,294,271 "
Hu-nan	12,705,728- "		12,705,728 "
Total	330,000,000 "	70,000,000 "	400,000,000 "

THE QUANTITY OF WHEAT AND WHITE RICE REQUIRED TO BE TRANSPORTED TO PEKING

Province	Wheat due to the Peking Granary	Wheat due to the *Peh-tung-chow* Granary	White rice due to both granaries
Shang-tung ...	991,576 *sinc*	939,170 *sinc*	
Ho-nan	2,465,278 "	1,276,696 "	
Kiang-su [1] ...			15,043,847 *sinc*
Che-Kiang [1] ..			6,620,000 "
Total	3,456,854 "	2,215,866 "	21,663,847 "

[1] The white rice paid in *Kiang-su* was really required from only four prefectures, *viz., Soo-chow, Sung-kiang, Siang-chow* and *Tai-chong*; and that paid in *Che-kiang*, from two prefectures, *viz., Tsa-sing* and *Hu-chow*.

canal transportation. Still in the first decade of the twentieth century one hundred million *sinc* of rice from *Kiang-su* and *Che-kiang* were transported from Shanghai to Tientsin by steamers every year, because the cost of transportation was reasonable.

BEAN AND SILVER SUBSTITUTES FOR THE REQUIRED RICE

Province.	Quantity of black beans substituted for equal quantity of rice.[1]	Quantity of white rice for which other rice might be substituted.[2]	Quantity of rice for which silver was always substituted.[3]	Quantity of rice deducted from the original quantity as exemption since 1865.	Quantity of rice substituted for lime.[4]
	sinc	*sinc*	*sinc*	*sinc*	*sinc*
Shan-tung	11,319,655	....	7,000,000	....	....
Ho-nan	9,616,985	....	7,000,000	....	....
Kiang-su	....	8,141,347	10,649,269	54,312,600	2,942,422
Che-kiang	....	3,622,500	....	26,676,500	4,807,740
An-hwei	....	....	7,596,131	....	....
Hu-peh	....	....	3,252,060	....	....
Hu-nan	....	....	521,205	....	....
Total	20,936,640	11,763,847	36,018,665	80,989,100	7,750,162

[1] In the first column, the quantity of black beans varied more or less directly with the quantity of rice in the Peking Granary.

[2] In the second column, the quantity of white rice to be exchanged was fixed.

[3] In the third column, the exchange rates between silver and rice were fixed according to the market prices in the provinces.

[4] In the fifth column, the quantity of rice, being substituted for a certain quantity of lime, was not deducted from the total quantity of rice or white rice as in case of the preceding columns; but was, in turn, replaced by a payment in silver. The rate was fixed as follows: 1.2 *tael* of silver = 100 *sinc* of rice.

MINIMUM AND MAXIMUM RATES [1] OF THE EXTRA CHARGE [2] ON THE
TRANSPORTED RICE

Province	Extra charge on every hundred *sinc* of rice due to the Peking Granary	Extra charge on every hundred *sinc* of rice to the *Peh-tung-chow* Granary
Shan-tung [3]	25 [6]	17
Ho-nan [3]	25 - 28	17
Kiang-su [4]	25 - 40	22 - 30
An-hwei	30 - 40	25 - 30
Kiang-si	40	40
Che-kiang [4]	40	40
Hu-peh [5]	40	
Hu-nan [5]	40	

TRANSPORTATION FEES [7]

Province	Payments with every hundred *sinc* of rice due to the Peking Granary		Payments with every hundred *sinc* of rice due to the *Peh-tung-chow* Granary
	in silver	in rice	in rice
Shan-tung	.05 *tael*	21 *sinc*	
Ho-nan	.05 "	21 "	
An-hwei	.05 "	31 "	2 *sinc*
Kiang-su (North)	.05 "	31 "	2 "
Kiang-su (South)	.1 "	31 "	2 "
Che-kiang	.34 "	36 "	2 "
Kiang-si	.03 "	52 "	2 "
Hu-peh	....	56 "	
Hu-nan	....	56 "	

[1] See *The Amendments of the Institutes of the Tsing Dynasty*, chs. cxciv-cxcvii.

[2] For the extra charge, see *supra*, p. 37.

[3] *Shan-tung* and *Ho-nan* paid to these granaries wheat and beans at the same rates of extra charge.

[4] The rates of extra charge on every hundred *sinc* of white rice were thirty *sinc* in *Kiang-su* and forty *sinc* in *Che-kiang*.

[5] *Hu-peh* and *Hu-nan* had no rice due to the *Peh-tung-chow* Granary.

[6] Figures are in *sinc* per one hundred *sinc* of the transported rice.

[7] This table does not include the collection fees which were determined by the district magistrates.

Balance of Expenditures and Revenues

The financial history of the *Tsing* Dynasty, 1644-1911, may be divided into two periods by the Chino-Japanese War, 1894-5. The former period, 1644-1893, may be called normal, because revenues were generally sufficient to meet expenditures in a systematic manner. Although expenditures grew larger during the last five decades of this period due to the *Tai-ping* Rebellion of 1850-1864, and the intercourse with foreign countries, yet they could be made up by new sources of revenues. For instance, the total revenues of 1887 were in excess of the total expenditures of the same year:

```
Total revenues  ................................... 78,515,215 taels
Total expenditures  ................................ 67,448,649   "

    Balance  ...................................... 11,066,566   "
```

If we differentiate both the total revenues and the total expenditures into old and new, we have the following figures:

```
Old revenues from land, salt, regular customs ........ 42,448,915 taels
Old expenditures,
    Permanent appropriations ......... 32,129,683 taels
    Temporary appropriations ........  8,733,791   "     40,863,474   "

    Balance ....................................... 1,585,441   "

New revenues from maritime customs and li-kin duty 36,066,300 taels
New expenditures for new army and navy, cost of col-
    lecting new revenues and redemption of foreign debts 26,585,175   "

    Balance ....................................... 9,481,125   "
```

Then we pass to the latter period, 1894-1911, which is abnormal in the sense that the government of the *Tsing* Dynasty would have become bankrupt before the Revolu-

tion of 1911 were it not for foreign loans.[1] This condition
was brought about by the Chino-Japanese War of 1894-5,
the Boxer Disturbance of 1900 and the reforms of government, 1906-1911. The growth of expenditures and revenues of this period may be learned from the first Chinese
budget of 1911. This budget was made in 1910 by the Department of Finance based on the estimates of expenditures
of the different *yâmens* at Peking and the provinces, and on
the average sum of annual incomes of 1908-9, as reported
by the investigators, sent to the provinces by the Department of Finance in 1909, and by other authorities. Although its operation has been interfered with by the Revolution of 1911, it furnishes the most reliable information
concerning the financial condition on the eve of the Revolution.

PUBLIC REVENUES [2] FOR 1911

Land Tax		48,101,346.273 *taels*
(a) Ordinary	46,312,355.022 *taels*	
(b) Incidental	1,936,656.421 "	
Salt Taxes		46,312,355.022 "
Maritime Customs Duties		35,139,917.965 "
Regular Customs Duties		6,999,369.966 "
(a) Ordinary	6,990,845.925 "	
(b) Incidental	8,524.041 "	
Miscellaneous Taxes		26,163,842.177 "
Li-kin Duty		43,187,907.099 "
Public Industries [3]		46,600,899.753 "
Incidental Contributions		5,652,333.117 "
Miscellaneous Incomes		35,244,750.650 "
Internal Debt		3,560,000.000 "
Total		296,962,722.022 "

[1] For the amount of foreign loans see H. B. Morse, *The Trade and Administration of the Chinese Empire* (New York, 1908).

[2] *Cf. infra*, p. 44, note 1.

[3] The public industries, excluding railways and telegraphs, are different in different provinces. The most common one is the mint.

PUBLIC EXPENDITURES [1] FOR 1911

Foreign intercourse	3,544,732.977 *taels*
Police administration	4,227,563.742 "
Public ceremonies	792,127.940 "
Financial administration	28,130,434.754 "
Palace and imperial household	6,144,877.170 "
The Council of State and other departments	6,348,826.271 "
Provincial administration	19,822,730.489 "
National Assembly [2]	786,666.666 "
Public debt redemption and interest	56,413,576.498 "
Public industries [3]	5,600,435.211 "
Public education	3,375,474.756 "
Army and its supplies	126,743,333.389 "
Navy and its supplies	10,503,202.794 "
Administration of justice	7,716,016.765 "
Administration of agriculture, industry and commerce	2,040,003,373 "
Public works	4,515,271.832 "
Administration of railways and telegraphs	55,141,906.832 "
Government of dependencies	1,705,103.877 "
Total national expenditures	338,652,295.073 "
Local expenditures	37,703,362.170 "
Grand total	376,355,657.243 "

General Features of Expenditure and Revenue

The most striking features of the period under consideration may be classified as follows: (1) the general characteristics throughout the *Tsing* Dynasty, 1644-1911; (2) the special characteristic of the earlier period, 1644-1893; and (3) the special characteristic of the later period, 1894-1911. The general characteristics consist of two points. One is the improper division of income among the different governmental agencies. For instance, at least one-third of

[1] These tables of expenditures and revenues are abstracted from the original budget submitted by the Department of Finance, not from the final budget modified by the National Assembly. They represent the actual needs of the government rather than the final appropriations.

[2] The National Assembly was created in 1910.

[3] *Cf. supra,* p. 43, note 3.

the total income was spent for military purposes, while the total local expenditures or the reserved fund, as it was called, was small compared with the amount needed for local improvements. Another point is that the important forms of taxation remained unchanged during all these years. The special characteristic of the earlier period is the transportation of revenues, in the form of silver or product, due to the lack of development of commerce; and that of the later period is the development of numerous forms of incomes in the different provinces, termed the miscellaneous incomes, the most undesirable forms of which may be mentioned as follows:

(1) The so-called contribution. This was simply a euphonious term used for the receipts from the sale of public offices. A person might become a candidate for an office by contributing a certain sum of money. The highest office which could be bought in this way was the circuit governorship in the provinces and the office of a first-class secretary in the department at Peking. This source, yielding a gross return of 5,652,333.117 *taels* according to the budget of 1911, was found in Peking and all the provinces subject to the control of the Department of Finance which issued the official diplomas.

(2) The gambling tax. In *Kwang-tung* Province this tax was advanced in a lump sum by a company which had a monopoly of all the gambling houses in Canton, the capital of *Kwang-tung*. According to the budget of 1911, this source yielded about 4,400,000 *taels,* forming one-eighth of the total amount of miscellaneous incomes of the country. As compared with the returns of the other important sources of revenues in the same province, it took a third place. The receipts ran as follows: maritime customs duties, 6,103,610 *taels; li-kin* duty, 5,046,256 *taels;* gambling tax, 4,400,-

ooo *taels;* salt monopoly, 2,417,597 *taels;* public industries, 2,372,986 *taels;* and land tax, 1,803,637 *taels.*

(3) The lottery monopolies in *Hu-peh, Kiang-su* and other provinces. The *Hu-peh lottery* was a government monopoly, while the lotteries in *Kiang-su* and other provinces were monopolized by private companies, each paying a franchise tax to the respective provincial governments. But the lottery of one province might be sold in any other province. The income from this source amounted to several million *taels.*

CHAPTER III

Taxation of Land [1]

The Revolution of 1911 affected only slightly the general system of taxation in China and consequently the following description of conditions as they existed during the *Tsing* Dynasty may be accepted as a substantially accurate account of the present situation.

The land tax has been playing the most important rôle among all the sources of revenue. It owes its importance both to the economic condition and to the historical development. In order to describe the present system of taxing land, it is necessary to treat separately the land system, the land policy, the tax system, the land rent, the exemption of payment, the rates and the administrative rules.

The Land System

The agricultural lands of the whole country liable to pay a tax or rent consist of nine principal classes:

(A) The People's Lands are those which are the private property of the people and subject to sale or purchase at their own will.

(B) The Changed-name Lands are those which were owned by the absent nobles of the *Ming* Dynasty, 1368-1644, and transferred with property rights to the people of the respective districts in which they are situated.

(C) The Soldier-cultivated Lands are those given to the soldiers to be cultivated in vacation, *i. e.*, in time when they are not called on for the periodical drilling, the capture of

---

[1] For the Chinese systems of measure and weight, see Appendix A.

robbers and the transportation of grain to Peking and its vicinity. Since 1650, owing to the organization of regular forces in the different provinces, the farming soldiers are no longer actual soldiers except those engaged in transporting grain, and their lands are taxed by the civil authorities.

(D) The Horse-breeding Lands are those which were originally enclosed for horse-breeding in *Chi-li, Shan-si, Kan-su* and certain cities in other provinces, but now in the hands of the people for cultivation.

(E) The Weed-growing Lands are the marshes found in the maritime provinces, such as, *Kiang-su, Kiang-si, Hu-peh* and *Hu-nan*.

(F) The Villa Lands are those whose rents, paid in product, flow into the treasury of the Department of Palace Affairs. They are situated in *Chi-li* and *Feng-tien* Provinces.

(G) The Banner Lands are those given to the soldiers to be cultivated for their own use. They are generally found in *Moukden* (Manchuria) and near Peking, and are not allowed to be sold or mortgaged.

(H) The Public Lands are those held by the government. The different provinces use the revenues from these lands for different purposes.

(I) The Education Lands are those whose incomes go to the provincial treasuries for educational expenses.

The Land Policy

Of the nine classes of cultivated lands, only the first was being cultivated by the owners themselves or their tenants at the beginning of the *Tsing* Dynasty, 1644-1911, when the other eight classes were public domains. As the Chinese land policy is to develop agriculture in the country, the government tries to put every tract of land available for agriculture into cultivation by a free disposal of lands to the people.   As the result of this policy the area of public tillable lands put into cultivation was calculated in 1887 to be 186,495,407 *mou*.   Practically all of these lands, cleared by virtue of imperial grants, were turned into private properties by those who had cleared them.   The total area of lands retained by the government and rented to the tenants in order to secure revenues for specific purposes is comparatively small.   The existing public cultivated lands are now known as the Villa Lands, the Education Lands, the Public Lands in general and the Banner Lands.

AREA OF CULTIVATED LANDS IN 1887

Province	Area [1] of Lands in *Mou*.
Chi-li	69,254,823
Feng-tien	26,554,229
Ki-rin	1,429,214
Shan-tung	125,931,405
Ho-nan	71,675,185
Shan-si	56,476,803
An-hwei	41,113,028
Kiang-su	110,825,370
Kiang-si	47,341,581
Fu-kien	13,400,056
Che-kiang	46,770,515
Hu-peh	117,322,955
Hu-nan	34,874,255
Shen-si	30,591,330
Kan-su	16,775,160
Sze-chuen	46,415,898
Kwang-tung	34,730,825
Kwang-si	8,963,783
Turkestan	11,480,191
Total in the report of 1887	911,976,606
Yun-nan [2] in the report of 1853	9,319,360
Kwei-chow [2] in the report of 1812	2,765,025
Grand total	924,060,991

[1] *The Institutes of the Tsing Dynasty*, 5th edition, (Shanghai, 1909), ch. xvii.

[2] *Yun-nan* and *Kwei-chow* sent their latest reports in 1853 and 1812 respectively.

AREA OF PUBLIC AND PRIVATE CULTIVATED LANDS IN 1887, SHOWING THE
RESULT OF THE LAND POLICY

Province	Area of private land [1]	Area of public land [5]
Chi-li [2]	68,332,031 *mou*	972,792 *mou*
Feng-tien	5,239,889 "	21,314,340 "
Ki-rin	1,429,214 "	
Shan-tung	123,600,758 "	2,330,647 "
Shan-si	47,918,531 "	8,558,272 "
Ho-nan	62,766,216 "	8,908,969 "
Kiang-su	65,757,338 "	45,068,032 "
An-hwei	34,063,630 "	7,049,398 "
Kiang-si	46,176,300 "	1,165,281 "
Fu-kien	12,601,238 "	798,818 "
Che-kiang	44,713,511 "	2,057,004 "
Hu-peh [2]	58,102,760 "	59,220,195 "
Hu-nan [2]	31,304,200 "	3,570,055 "
Shen-si [2]	25,797,024 "	4,794,306 "
Kan-su	9,196,385 "	7,578,775 "
Sze-chuen [2]	46,415,898 "	
Kwang-tung	34,193,764 "	537,061 "
Kwang-si [2]	8,963,783 "	
Turkestan [4]		11,480,191 "
Total	726,572,470 "	185,404,136 "
Yun-nan [3]	8,394,238 "	925,122 "
Kwei-chow [3]	2,598,876 "	166,149 "
Grand total	737,565,584 "	186,495,407 "

[1] By "Private Land" is meant the People's Land while all the other classes are included in public land because of their origin.

[2] It is often found in the provincial reports that the different classes of land are not separately calculated, there being a failure to distinguish not only between various classes of public lands, but also between the private and public lands, *e. g.*, the area of private lands in *Chi-li, Hu-peh* and *Sze-chuen* includes the Soldier-cultivated lands; that in *Hu-nan*, the Changed-name Lands; that in *Kwang-si*, the public lands; that in *Shen-si*, the Education Lands.

[3] *Yun-nan* and *Kwei-chow* did not send their reports in 1887. The figures for the former are taken from the report of 1853, and those for the latter, from the report of 1812.

[4] Turkestan's figure denotes the area of public lands in a few cities, while the whole territory is practically uncultivated.

[5] Thousands of *mou* of public cultivated lands are believed not to be

GRADUAL INCREASE OF CULTIVATED LANDS SHOWING THE RESULT OF THE
LAND POLICY [1]

Year	Area of Land
1661	549,357,600 *mou*
1685	607,843,000 "
1722	683,791,400 "
1766	741,449,500 "
1812	791,525,100 "
1833	742,000,000 "
1887	911,976,606 "

[1] The figures are taken from Tang Shou Chien, *Inquiry into the Institutions of China* (Shanghai), bk. iii, ch. i.

The Tax System

(A) The Compound Land Tax.

The compound land tax at present is composed of five elements:

(a) The Regular Land Tax.

(b) The Poll Tax.

(c) The General Personal Service Money.

(d) The Post Station Money.

(e) The Compensatory Tax.

(a) The Regular Land Tax. Since 594 B. C. the land has been taxed by *mou* (acreage), *i. e.*, a tax has been levied on each *mou* of land. From 770 to the present time there has been no uniform rate proportional to the amount of gross produce. Owing to the fact that the old method of assessment was abandoned without the introduction of a new method, the rates to-day are fixed merely by tradition.[1] The tax was originally paid in produce. Since 1436 it has been paid partly in silver and partly in produce. This change is not an attempt to approximate more closely the

included in this table due either to no report or to the calculation with local standards of measure. Unfortunately, these are the only reliable figures. They are taken from the latest (5th) edition of *The Institutes of the Tsing Dynasty*, ch. xvii.

[1] For the rates in force at present, *cf. infra*, pp. 56-64.

tax-paying ability of the land-holder; the amounts, collected year by year, have not increased or decreased so that each person contributes approximately the same as before.

(b) The Poll Tax.   The poll tax was levied during the early years of the *Tsing* Dynasty, 1644-1911, upon several classes of people, namely, the urban people, the country people, the rich people, the tenants and the immigrants from other localities.   Each of these was further classified under three grades according to their ability to pay.   The age of a person was also taken into consideration because an adult, *i. e.*, sixteen years old, was regarded as having greater ability than a child.   A census was published every five years in order to correct the errors regarding population.   This method of assessment was soon found impracticable, due to the lack of accurate reports of increasing members of the individual families.   In 1713, Emperor Kang-shi ordered that the census of 1711 should be taken as a standard and the increased population be exempted from taxation.

During the period 1716-1793 the poll taxes of different provinces were amalgamated with the land taxes, except in *Feng-tien*, twenty districts of *Shan-si* and the greater part of *Kwei-chow*.   The poll tax was originally levied in China on the assumption of an equal distribution of lands in a primitive society.   With the increase of population, the scarcity of land and the unequal distribution of lands among the population, the poll tax has lost its value as a test of ability to pay.[1]   Whereas land is the dominant source of wealth in an agricultural community, the only way for the Chinese government to make good the loss of revenue from the poll tax was to raise the rates of land taxes as she did in the process of amalgamation.   Therefore, we may consider this modification of the tax system as an advance step towards the goal of ability to pay in taxation.

[1] Tang Shou Chien, *Inquiry into the Institutions of China*, bk. iii, ch. iii, p. 3.

(c) The General Personal-Service Money. All kinds of public service were formerly done with forced labor. It was the duty of everybody to serve in this way without payment. Later, money was paid instead of service, and with it voluntary laborers were employed. This commutation tax has been also amalgamated with the land tax in order to save the trouble of collection.

(d) The Post-Station Money. Aside from the post-office, China has been providing her own means of communication known as the post stations established throughout the Empire especially for military and other public purposes. The service was formerly performed by the people. It is now paid for out of the public treasury, while the people are required to pay a tax known as the Post-Station Money which is collected with the land tax.

(e) The Compensatory Tax. Besides the regular taxes and the commutation taxes, there is a compensatory tax which is so called because it was originally an illegal charge by the magistrates for the compensation of loss of silver from melting. At the beginning of the *Tsing* Dynasty, 1644-1911, the practice was strictly prohibited by the following laws:[1]

(1) The Imperial Decree of 1644 announcing that the imposition of " melting loss " shall be punished as bribery.

(2) The Law of 1665 permitting the people to complain of any sort of excessive charges before the courts.

(3) The Law of 1678 holding liable the provincial high officials for the concealment of the guilt of subordinates levying the " melting loss ".

But the practice could not be checked because the government did not provide adequate revenues for the districts, nor sufficient salaries for the magistrates, as it was said by

---

[1] Wang Ching Yun, *Essays on the Institutions of the Tsing Dynasty* (Shanghai, 1901), ch. iii.

Emperor Kang Shi in a decree of 1709. This decree is a reply to Mr. Loo-yu, the governor of *Ho-nan,* saying, " It is impossible for any magistrate to support his family and to pay for the services rendered by his secretaries and servants, without charging a single cash in excess. A magistrate charging ten per cent in excess of the regular taxes may be considered as a good official. If he were not excused from impeachment, it seems to me, it would be irksome for you to inflict the same penalty on so many of your subordinates." Then the rates of the compensatory taxes in the different provinces were ten per cent of the regular taxes or less, *i. e.,* one *mace*[1] per *tael* of regular taxes; but the rates in *Hu-nan* were twenty per cent or thirty per cent. In 1722, the rates in *Shen-si* varied from twenty per cent to fifty per cent of the regular taxes when the provincial treasury incurred a deficit. The governor asked Emperor Kang Shi's permission to take the collected revenues from the compensatory tax out of the magistrates' pockets; but the Emperor refused, because he thought his permission would mean the confirmation of the charge of the illegal tax. In 1724, the Governor of *Shan-si* requested the legalization of the compensatory tax to meet the deficit of that province. Emperor Yung-tsing granted this request on the condition that the compensatory tax should be abolished whenever the public revenues shall be found adequate. From that time on one province after another followed the precedence of *Shan-si.* This source of revenue is now appropriated for official salaries and local purposes.

The Land Rent

As we have seen that the government nominally owns at present only four classes of public cultivated lands, we now

---

[1] Ten *maces* are equal to one *tael*.

come to discuss how the government deals with such lands. First, the Villa Lands are leased to the tenants who pay rice to the Department of Palace Affairs as rent. In the second place, the Banner Lands are either given to the Tartar soldiers under the Eight Banners without any kind of payment, or leased to the Chinese tenants in order to secure rents in money for some other soldiers who have no land. These two classes of lands, therefore, are not subject to the taxing power of the Department of Finance. Finally, the other two classes of public lands which are under the control of the Department of Finance are known as the Education Lands for educational expenses, and the Public Lands in general for other public purposes of the provinces. Rates of rents derived from these lands are fixed by law and are not accommodated to the fluctuation of economic rents. The privilege of the tenants is the exemption from payment of all other burdens, that is to say, the poll tax, the General Personal Service Money, the Post-Station Money and the Compensatory Tax.

The Exemption of Payments

The following classes of uncultivated land are exempt from the payment of taxes:

(a) The Forbidden Lands are not open to cultivation, because their low productivity is supposed to yield less return that the expense of cultivation.

(b) The Scattered Lands are those scattered in small pieces. The exemption is subject to certain limitations, such as fertility, size or location, *i. e.*, on mountain or near river bank.

(c) The Exempt Lands are those which are used as sites for the buildings or are rented in order to augment the revenues for public worship, public education and public charity.

(d) The Unmeasured Lands are occupied by various barbarous tribes in *Sze-chuen, Yun-nan* and *Kan-su* Provinces.   In lieu of the land tax, each family of these tribes pays a poll tax.

(e) The Hunting Lands are those used for hunting game in Manchuria.

(f) The Nomadic Lands consist of Mongolia, Turkestan and other districts near to them, where the nomadic tribes wander from place to place in search of pasture or game.

Existing Rates

The rates of the regular land tax and the land rent vary to a greater or less extent in different provinces, or even in different places of the same province.   They are also different according to the various classes of land and the various kinds of agricultural products.   This differentiation is based upon suppositions as to the productivity of land and the density of population.[1]   There is no scientific measure of productivity by the modern method of valuation, nor accurate census of population.   But it must be known that the determination of land fertility by the color of soil may be traced back from the *Hsia* Dynasty, 2205-1766 B. C., when the available lands were cultivated earlier or later according to their superiority of productive power and the number of immobile laborers already there.   On the other hand, the compensatory taxes are levied in the different provinces at certain fixed rates per *tael* of the regular taxes. In some cases these rates are uniform throughout the whole province; while in others they are different or exempt as determined by the customary practices in the different localities.   To prevent confusion there have been included, in the subjoined tables, only the minimum and maximum rates in the different provinces, ignoring the variation[2] between these limits.

---

[1] Tang Shou Chien, *Inquiry into the Institutions of China*, bk. iii, ch. i, p. 2.

[2] *The Comprehensive Book of Taxation and Service of the Tsing Dynasty* (Peking) contains the full text.

MINIMUM AND MAXIMUM RATES OF THE REGULAR TAX ON EACH MOU OF THE PEOPLE'S LAND

Province.	Silver.	Rice.	Beans.	Wheat.
	tael	*sinc*	*sinc*	*sinc*
Chi-li	(.0081)-(.13+)	(1)-(10+)	(.9008)-(4+)	....
Feng-tien ...	(.01)-(.02+)	(2.08)-(7.5+)	....	....
Ki-rin[1]	(.01)-(.03)	(2.2)-(6.6)	....	....
Shan-tung ...	(.0032)-(.1091+)	(.02)-(3.06+)	....	(.001)-(.43+)
Shan-si	(.00107)-(.1+)	(.15)-(27+)	....	....
Ho-nan	(.0014)-(.227+)	(.07)-(2.2+)	....	....
An-hwei[2] ...	(.015)-(.106+)	(.21)-(7.1+)	(.08)-(.91+)	(.05)-(.08+)
Kiang-si[2] ...	(.001336)-(.117013)	(.14)-(10.7205+)	....	....
Fu-kien	(.0169)-(.1625+)	(.0109)-(2.47+)	....	....
Che-kiang[2] ..	(.01503)-(.255+)	(.003)-(19+)	....	....
Hu-peh[3]	(.2545)-(2.9741+)	(.0006)-(29.1408+)	....	....
Hu-nan[3]	(.20238)-(1.8404+)	(.0209)-(14.69+)	....	....
Shen-si[3]	(1.059)-(2.773+)	(.01)-(10.16+)	....	....
Kiang-su[2] ...	(.009)-(.1411+)	(1.47)-(19.26+)	Included in rice.	(.0002)-(.03+)
Kan-su	(.0002)-(.1504+)	(.03)-(8.11+)	....	....
Sze-chuen ...	(.00159)-(.08491+)	......	....	....
Kwang-tung.	(.0081)-(.2232+)	(.65)-(2.29+)	....	....
Kwang-si....	(.0204)-(.2122+)	(3.7)-(5.35+)	....	....
Yun-nan	(.0055)-(.0465+)	(1.94)-(15+)	....	....
Kwei-chow ..	(.01)-(.65+)	(.5001)-(45+)	1.0	....

[1] In *Ki-rin* the required rice may be paid in silver, the exchange rate being 100 *sinc* rice = 1 *tael* silver.

[2] In *Kiang-su, An-hwei, Kiang-si* and *Che-kiang*, there are two sorts of the People's Land,—the low land, called '*Tien*' (field) and the high land, called '*Ti*' (ground)—paying different rates of tax. The figures in the table indicate the rates on each *mou* of low land. The rates on each *mou* of high land are as follows: Kiang-su .009-.3303 *tael* silver, .73-41.69 *sinc* rice and bean, .001-.08 *sinc* wheat; An-hwei, .0089-.63 *tael* silver, .79-5.9 *sinc* rice, .08-.22 *sinc* wheat; Kiang-si, .000054-.211128 *tael* silver, .052-5.128 *sinc* rice; Che-kiang, .0024-.2132 *tael* silver, .008-19.35 *sinc* rice.

[3] In *Hu-peh, Hu-nan* and *Shen-si* only rice is required to be paid. If the payment of silver is preferred, the rates in the "silver" column of this table are the exchange rates for every 100 *sinc* of rice.

MINIMUM AND MAXIMUM RATES OF THE REGULAR TAX ON EACH MOU
OF THE SOLDIER-CULTIVATED LAND

Province	Class[1]	Silver		Rice[2]	
Chi-li[3]	A	.00072–.0793	*tael*	.897–9.072	*sinc*
Shan-tung	A	.01–.065	"	......	
Shan-tung	B	.01–.0538	"	......	
Shan-si	A	.0023–.014	"	1.08–10.9	"
Shan-si	B	.014	"	......	
Ho-nan	A	.0016–.108	"	......	
Kiang-su[4]	A	.009–.1411	"	1.47–19.26	"
An-hwei	A	.01–.06	"	1.8–8.6	"
An-hwei	B	.0179–2.7229	"	.3–25.41	"
Kiang-si[5]	A( )	.502975–.548384	"	3.959–27.3	"
Kiang-si[5]	A(2)	.2	"	7.973–22.803	"
Kiang-si[5]	A(3)	.04166	"	......	
Kiang-si[5]	A(4)	.090047–.114245	"	......	
Che-kiang	A	.00572–.149	"	15.75–24	"
Hu-peh	A	......		1.5–9.96	"
Hu-peh[6]	B	.3–1.3166	"	1.2–18	"
Hu-nan[7]	A	.0019–.1043	"	.38–20	"
Hu-nan[7]	B	.56	"	1–12.5	"
Shen-si	A	.002–.098	"	1.5–30	"
Kan-su	A	.0012–.006	"	5–6	"
Kan-su[8]	B	......		4.187	"
Sze-chuen	A	.0125–.3	"	27.27	"
Sze-chuen[9]	B	.0125–.02	"	1.929–80	"
Kwang-tung	A	.0081–.2232	"	8.88	"
Yun-nan	A	......		5.92–8.18	"
Kwei-chow[10]	A	.0141–.234	"	5.35–37.33	"

[1] Class A is under the administration of civil officials and class B, of military officers.

[2] The word "rice" indicates rice itself or together with other minor cereals.

[3] *Chi-li* also pays .438 to 3.6 *sinc* beans and .0192 to .0417 *tael* straw per *mou*.

[4] *Kiang-su* also pays .002 to .03 *sinc* wheat per *mou*.

[5] In *Kiang-si*, class A(1) indicates low land; class A(2), high land; class A(3), fractional land; and class A(4), a substitute for the non-existence of the Soldier-cultivated Land in *Fu-kien*. Only rice is required from class A(1), and class A(2). If the silver payment is preferred, the figures under the "silver" column are the exchange rates for every 100 *sinc* of rice.

[6] In *Hu-peh*, only rice is required from class B. If the payer pre-

MINIMUM AND MAXIMUM RATES OF THE REGULAR TAX ON EACH MOU
OF THE CHANGED-NAME LAND

Province	Silver	Rice [1]
Chi-li	.0053 - .1173 *tael*	*sinc*
Shan-tung [2]	.01 - .3007 "	1.8 "
Shan-si	.005 - .14 "	.07 - 20 "
Ho-nan	.011 - .129 "	
Hu-peh [3]	.466 "	.449 - 6.31 "
Hu-nan [3]	.3735 - .9244 "	.5 - 12 "
Shen-si	.0069 - .0751 "	4.35 - 14.8 "
Kan-su [4]	.0048 - .0171 "	.22 - 1.42 "

fers to pay silver, every 100 *sinc* of rice is considered as equivalent to the figure under the " silver " column.

[7] In *Hu-nan* class A pays both silver and rice which may be changed to silver (100 *sinc* rice = .1774 — 1.6531 *tael* silver), while class B pays only rice, the exchange rate of 100 *sinc* rice being included in the " silver " column.

[8] In *Kan-su*, class B pays .058 *tael* straw in addition to rice.

[9] In *Sze-chuen*, beans are paid together with rice and the figure under the " rice " column indicates the amount of both.

[10] *Kwei-chow* pays 30 *sinc* beans and 23.33 — 31.14 *sinc* wheat per *mou* besides the payment of silver and rice.

[1] The word " rice " indicates rice and other minor cereals.

[2] In *Shan-tung* wheat is required. The rate is .32 *sinc* per *mou*.

[3] In *Hu-peh* and *Hu-nan* only rice is required to be paid. If the silver payment is preferred, the rates in the " silver " column of this table are the exchange rates for every 100 *sinc* of rice.

[4] In *Kan-su* straw is required. The rate is .01-.092 *tael* per *mou*.

MINIMUM AND MAXIMUM RATES OF THE REGULAR TAX OR THE LAND
RENT ON EACH MOU OF THE SPECIAL CLASSES OF LANDS

(a) Chi-li

Class [1]	Silver	
The Mulberry Land	.00168	*tael*
The Foliage Crop Land	.05 - .7251	"
The Weed-growing Land [2]	.01 - .06	"
The Sand Deposit Land	.029 - .2565	"
The Education Land [3]	.01 - .2678	"

(b) Manchuria

Province	Class [4]	Silver	Produce	
Feng-tien	The Re-opened Land [5]	.01–.03 *tael*	4.3 –10 *sinc* bean [6]	
Feng-tien	The Illegally-cultivated Land [7]	.48 "	2.65 "	rice
Ki-rin	The Discovered Land [8]	.08 "	.442 "	rice [9]

[1] *Chi-li* has eight kinds of lands excluding the Banner Land and the Villa Land which are not under the administration of the magistrates. The rates of the three general classes are found in the foregoing tables. *Cf. supra*, pp. 57-59.

[2] This class is used as salt fields.

[3] The Education Land pays 6 *sinc* of wheat, corn and rice per *mou* besides silver.

[4] In addition to these classes both Feng-tien and Ki-rin have the People's Land mentioned above. *Cf. supra*, p. 57.

[5] The Re-opened Land is that first enclosed as the Banner Land and then re-opened to the cultivation of the common people.

[6] Of the amount of beans, a half is paid in kind and the other half, in silver, the exchange rate being 100 *sinc* beans = .6 *tael* silver.

[7] The Illegally-cultivated Land is that cultivated by the people without the property right conferred by the government.

[8] The Discovered Land is that illegally cultivated by the people who evade the tax until discovered.

[9] The rice is paid in silver. The exchange rate is: 100 *sinc* rice = 1 *tael* silver.

(c) Shan-tung

Class [1]		Silver
The Education Land	.009 - .3	*tael*
The Stove Land [2]	.0265 - .0441	"
The Changed-name Land under the military post [3]....	.00107 - .1	"

(d) Kiang-su

Class [4]	Silver	Rice and Beans	Wheat
The Hilly Land.......... The Weed-growing Land [5] The Swamp Land........	.009–.1405 *tael*....	.34–16.52 *sinc*....	.01–.03 *sine*
The City Ground [6]....... The Granary Ground [6].... The House Ground [6]......	.057–.1024 "	....5.05–12.63 "	....01–.02 "

(e) An-hwei

Class [7]	Silver	Rice	Wheat
The Pond or Water Land [8]	.019 - .044 *tael*	.47 - .78 *sinc*	.01 - .02 *sinc*
The Grass Hill [9]	.083	"	
The Mulberry Land [10]	.032	"	

[1] Shang-tung has six classes land. The three general classes are mentioned above. *Cf. supra*, pp. 57-59.

[2] The Stove Land also pays .01 - .41 *sinc* wheat and 1.8 - 2.84 *sinc* rice per *mou*.

[3] The former rates of this class were .006-.12 *tael*.

[4] *Kiang-su* has four classes of lands. The two general classes appear above. *Cf. supra*, pp. 57-58.

[5] This class is used as salt fields.

[6] This class is taxed according to the number of buildings. But it is not a tax on buildings or house tax.

[7] An-hwei has five classes of lands. We have given the two general classes above. *Cf. supra*, pp. 57-58.

[8] The tax on this class is estimated by *mou*. The figures indicate the rate per *mou*.

[9] This class yielding grass pays taxes according to the length of the land. The figure represnts the rate per *li*. *Li* is a Chinese standard measure of length, equivalent to 576 metres in the Metric System.

[10] The tax on this class is computed according to the weight of the finished goods (silk) of its produce (mulberry). Each *tael* of silk pays the above-mentioned sum, *i. e.*, .032 *tael*.

(f) Kiang-si

Class[1]	Silver	Rice
The Hilly Land	.000005 - .06276 *tael*	.017 - .1.418 *sinc*
The Pond or Water Land....	.000054 - .270677 "	.113 - 6.837 "

(g) Fu-kien

Class[2]		Silver
The Silver Payment Public Land [3]..........		.0087 - .4175 *tael*
The Education Land		.0643 - .6995 "

(h) Che-kiang

Class[4]	Silver	Rice
The Hilly Land	.00005 - .1963 *tael*	.006 - 5.37 *sinc*
The Weed-growing Land	.0004 - .073 "	.05 - 7.5 "
The Pond or Watery Land....	.0002 - .1245 "	.0007 - 1.68 "
The Lake-region Land	.0307 "	.095 "
The Mulberry Land[5]	.0019 - .0056 "	.001 "
The Tea Land [5]	.0015 "	.07 "
The Stove Land	.0161 - .1414 "	.37 - 3.7 "

(i) Kan-su

Class[6]	Silver	Cereals
The land under the military chiefs of the barbarous tribes [7]	.075 *tael*	2.425 *sinc*
The Fan tribes' land [8]		.4 - 3 "
The Animal-breeding Land	.006 "	

[1] *Kiang-si* has four classes of lands, the two general classes having been given above. *Cf. supra*, pp. 57-58.

[2] *Fu-kien* has only one general class of land as given above. *Cf. supra*, p. 57.

[3] This class consists of those lands left to the public by escheat or by absence of property owners. The payment is made with silver only.

[4] There are two general classes of lands in *Che-kiang*. *Cf. supra*, pp. 57-58.

[5] The rates on mulberry and tea are applied to each tree irrespective of the area of land.

[6] The three general classes of lands in *Kan-su* are mentioned above. *Cf. supra*, pp. 57-59.

[7] The barbarous tribes are governed by their own military chiefs, and their land, administered by them.

[8] This class nominally under the magistrates pays as the land tax .0215 - .03 *tael* straw together with the cereals per *mou*. In addition to this, each family pays a poll tax amounting to .3 *tael* silver and 10 - 25 *sinc* cereals.

(j) Hu-nan, Sze-chuen, Kwang-tung and Yun-nan

Province	Class [1]	Silver
Hu-nan ....The Mao tribes' land		.0015–.03679 *tael*
Sze-chuen ....The land under the military chiefs of the barbarous tribes...		.0034–.0231 "
Kwang-tung ....The sewages [2]........................		.04503 "
Kwang-tung .....The pools [2]........................		.394 "
Yun-nan ....The Horse Stable land [3].............		.02–.03 "
Yun-nan ....The Yi tribes' land..................		1 *sinc* cereals

(k) Kwang-si

Class [4]	Silver	Rice
The Public Land		6.42 - 20.77 *sinc*
The Yao tribes' Land		3 - 5.35 "
The Tung tribes' Land	.009 - .0223 *tael*	3.74 - 5.35 "
The Lang tribes' Land	.009 "	4.28 "
The Education Land	.009 "	24.84 "

(l) Kwei-chow

Class [5]	Silver	Rice
The land under the military chiefs of the barbarous tribes	.008 - .1 *tael*	.722 - 15 *sinc*
The Public Land		25 - 50 "
The Education Land [6]	.1 - .4 "	20 - 40 "
The Rent Land	.03 - .1 "	
The Hilly Land [7]................	.0136 - .05 "	5 "
The Worship Land [8]	.1 "	
The Famine-relief Land [9]		14.9 - 50 "

[1] The general classes of lands in these provinces may be found above. *Cf. supra*, pp. 57-59.

[2] The sewages or pools are taxed according to their number. The figure is the rate of tax on each one of them.

[3] The Horse-Stable Land was originally used for horse stables and later thrown open to cultivation.

[4] *Kwang-si* has only one general class, the People's Land, as mentioned above. *Cf. supra*, p. 57.

[5] *Kwei-chow* has two general classes of lands, see *supra*, pp. 71-74.

[6] This class also pays 20 - 110.78 *sinc* rice per *mou*.

[7] This class also pays 10 *sinc* wheat per *mou*.

[5] This class also pays 10 *sinc* beans per *mou*.

[9] This class also pays 4.13 - 125.12 *sinc* rice per *mou*.

MINIMUM AND MAXIMUM RATES OF THE COMPENSATORY TAX ADDED TO PER TAEL OF SILVER OF THE REGULAR TAX

Province	Minimum Rate	Maximum Rate	Uniform Rate
Chi-li [1]		.15 *tael*	
Feng-tien [1]			.1 *tael*
Shan-tung			.14 "
Shan-si [1]	.1 *tael*	.13 "	
Ho-nan	.1 "	.15 "	
Kiang-su	.05 "	.1 "	
An-hwei	.075 "	.1 "	
Kiang-si			.1 "
Fu-kien [1]			.1 "
Che-kiang	.04 "	.09 "	
Hu-peh			.11 "
Hu-nan			.1 "
Shen-si [1]			.15 "
Kan-su [1]			.15 "
Sze-chuen			.15 "
Kwang-tung [1]			.169 "
Kwang-si [1]	.08 "	.105 "	
Yun-nan [1]			.2 "
Kwei-chow [1]	.1 "	.15 "	

Administrative Rules

The administrative rules of the land tax are very complex. They may be described under three headings as follows:

(a) The Collector. The magistrate of a district is the only responsible collector within his jurisdiction. He may be recorded, promoted, degraded, or dismissed according to the amount of the tax assigned to his district which he succeeds in collecting. The general rule [2] is that a magistrate is recorded when he has collected the whole sum of one year, and promoted to a higher rank when he has done the same for three consecutive years. On the other hand,

---

[1] In *Ki-rin* and these ten provinces the compensatory tax is partly paid with rice. But it is too insignificant to be mentioned here.

[2] See *The Amendments of the Institutes of the Tsing Dynasty* (Shanghai, 1909), ch. clxxiii.

he is punished by postponing his promotion and forfeiting his annual salary, for a deferred payment of less than ten per cent of the assigned amount; by degrading him to one, two, three or four grades below his original rank, without removal from service, according to whether the deferred payment is ten per cent, twenty per cent, thirty per cent, or forty per cent; or by dismissing him from office for a deferred payment of fifty per cent or more. His supervisory officials [1] assume the joint responsibility and are subject to similar treatment. He, however, may recover his office by remitting the deferred payment while he remains in service by permission or while awaiting his successor. For this purpose, there are numerous limitations concerning the amount of deferred payment and the date of payment. No recovery is allowed, if a magistrate fails to pay to the public treasury forty per cent of the assigned tax for the three years from the date of his impeachment. In the case of deficit,[2] which is not due to the deferred payment of the people but due to the fraud, waste, or deferred payment of the magistrate himself, he is fined by the confiscation of his property with or without other punishments. His supervisory officials share his fine for the joint responsibility or bear it for the concealment of his deficit.

(b)   Method of Collection.[3]   The system of " single whip",[4] began to be established in 1581 and has been widely extended under the *Tsing* Dynasty, 1644-1911. This system requires the different elements of the compound

---

[1] *Cf. supra*, ch. i, p. 25.

[2] *Cf. The Amendments of the Institutes of the Tsing Dynasty,* ch. clxxv.

[3] The existing method was adopted in 1728.

[4] By this phrase, we mean that all kinds of imposition are simplified into a single item.

land tax, laid on each person, to be added together, and the amount to be collected in ten instalments. The amount of the tax, laid on each person, is estimated according to the quantity and class of his lands as entered in the " Surveyors' Book ". Before the beginning of every semi-annual collection, the magistrate provides ten detachable receipts, each with two duplicates, for each taxpayer. One of the two duplicates of each receipt is kept by the magistrate, and the other given to a policeman who informs the taxpayer, but does not collect the tax. Having been informed once or many times, the taxpayer is expected to put his tax in the " collecting box " of the district *yâmen*; and when he has done so, he is entitled to a receipt. The process is repeated until ten instalments have been paid. Every ten days the magistrate opens the box, counts the total amount, and reports it to his supervisory officials. The money collected in this manner has been wrapped up by the individual taxpayer; and if it is found less than the required amount, it is returned to the original payer and an entire repayment is demanded rather than a supplementary sum. This is done in order to prevent the fraud of exacting an illegal charge, however small. At the end of each semi-annual collection, the magistrate sends to the Executive Department a report and the entire collected revenue except a certain sum allowed to be deducted for the district expenditures.

(c) Periods of Collection. The tax is collected in two periods of the year. This system was established in 780 by Yang Yen, a prime minister in the *Tang* Dynasty, 618-907, and is known as the "two taxes", or the "summer and autumn taxes ". It has the same object as the " single whip " system, being the most important reform in the taxation system from Yang Yen's time to the present day. The summer tax is now collected from the second to the fifth month; and the autumn tax, from the eighth to the eleventh month. These periods are universal to all except five provinces. The periods of *Kwang-tung* are from the seventh to the eighth month of a year, and from the twelfth to the first month of the next year. *Yun-nan* and *Kwei-chow* are permitted to collect taxes from the ninth to the twelfth month of a year and from the first to the third month of the next year, while *Shen-si* and *Sze-chuen* have their own periods in the year, namely, from the second to the seventh month and from the eighth to the twelfth month. These changes of periods are due to the differences of climate necessary for the staple products of those provinces.

(d) The Auditing of Accounts. With the exception of a sum reserved for local purposes, the collected revenues are transported to the provincial treasury immediately after the close of each collecting period. At the end of a year, the circuit governor and the prefect are ordered to audit the accounts of their subordinate magistrates, such as the reserved fund, the transporting fund, the collected fund and the amount of deferred payment, and to report the result of investigation to the governor. Next year two copies of the provincial accounts of these items are sent to Peking, one to the Department of Finance to be audited, and the other to the Emperor. These reports must reach Peking before the fourth, fifth or sixth month according to the distance of the respective provinces from Peking.

General Features of the Land Tax

The general features of the land tax which are worthy of observation are:

(1) The considerable amount contributed by this source to the annual revenues. Before the creation of the maritime customs duties and the *li-kin* duties in the middle of

the nineteenth century, when the amount of the annual revenues was less than five million *taels,* the land tax formed two-thirds or more of the whole, while in the last few years before the Chino-Japanese War, 1894, it supplied about three-eighths of the total annual return of about eighty million *taels.*[1] In recent years it has constituted one-fourth of the annual tax revenue of a little over two hundred million *taels.*[2]

(2) This important part of the revenue is inelastic. For centuries, the amount apportioned has not been changed, and to do so would be extremely difficult. Nevertheless, this method has the advantage of securing a total fixed sum.

(3) The land tax is levied on the land without allowances for indebtedness.

(4) As the land tax has existed for centuries, the process of capitalization has proceeded to the point where the greater part of the burden has been eliminated. The persons who have lost by its establishment are not the same as those who own the lands at present. For the same reason, the question of equality and that of certainty are not of particular moment.

(5) Although the greater part of the land tax has been capitalized, yet there are some few uncertain elements which cannot be included in the calculations. Prominent among such elements is the depreciation of copper coins. As the tax is collected in terms of silver which is always scarce, the taxpayer must pay more copper coins for the same weight of silver owing to the depreciation. This means in effect an additional tax. This new element is

---

[1] During the 19th century the legal amount of land tax is over 31,000,000 *taels*. Annual variations are not great.

[2] According to the budget of 1911, the land tax revenue is 48,101,346 *taels*.

borne by the immediate taxpayer, so far as any portion of pure economic rent is held by him, when the action of competition is not found in full force, otherwise the burden is passed to the landlord. For this reason, the taxpayer always prefers to pay produce,[1] and the object of commuting produce to silver is hardly attained. Nevertheless, the method of commutation is now carried out in an irksome manner, because the magistrate is required to sell the produce on his own account, and to pay the required amount of silver to the government. It is evident that the magistrate suffers for the people. But the shrewd magistrates often escape the requirement or compensate themselves in other ways. One of the most important causes of discontent in recent years is the practice, indulged in by many governors, of coining as many copper coins as possible and circulating them in the whole country for the purpose of securing seigniorage.

(6) The cost of collection is very low, because the administration is vested in the district magistrates. Moreover, the method of collection is rather convenient.

---

[1] It will be recalled that a part of the land tax may be paid in produce or silver, but the other part must be paid in silver.

CHAPTER IV

Taxation of Salt [1]

Production of Salt

(1) General considerations. Salt is one of the most valuable products of China. It may be classified into three kinds, namely, sea salt, lake salt, and well salt. The first is produced in *Feng-tien, Chi-li, Shan-tung, Kiang-su, Che-kiang, Fu-kien* and *Kwang-tung* Provinces; the second, in *Shan-si, Shen-si* and *Kan-su* Provinces; and the third, in *Sze-chuen* and *Yun-nan* Provinces.

There are three methods of production, known as "field-drying", "board-drying" and "pan-drying." The field-drying means that the salt water on the fields is allowed to become dry on exposure to the sun, as in *Feng-tien, Chi-li, Shan-tung, Fu-kien, Kwang-tung, Shan-si, Shen-si, Kan-su* and that part of *Kiang-su* north of the *Hwai* River. The board-drying means to let the salt water evaporate on the boards exposed to the sun. This is used in *Che-kiang* and that part of *Kiang-su* which lies south of the *Hwai* River. The pan-drying means to heat the salt water in pans with fire, as in *Sze-chuen, Yun-nan, Che-kiang* and that part of *Kiang-su,* south of the *Hwai* River.

The quality of the salts so produced differs greatly. The field-dried salt is the best and is most in demand. Of the other two, the pan-dried salt is better than the board-dried salt. Some of the *Sze-chuen* salt, but not all, is exceedingly

[1] For the Chinese systems of measure and weight, *cf.* appendix A.

white and pure, while the lake salt in *Shan-si, Shen-si* and *Kan-su* generally has a green color and an unpleasant taste.

The cost of production varies with the production methods. The field-dried salt is the cheapest. One *catty* of salt costs less than one-tenth of one cent in time of plenty, like May and June. Even in other months of the year, one *catty* of salt is sold for not more than three-tenths of one cent. The cost of both the pan-dried salt and the board-dried salt is higher. It varies from four-tenths or five-tenths of one cent to one cent for one *catty*. The best of the *Sze-chuen* salt (pan-dried) costs even more than one cent for one *catty*. The average cost for one *catty* of salt, however, is less than five-tenths of one cent because more than half of the total annual product is made up of field-dried salt.

(2) The quantity of product. The quantity of product is fixed by law on the assumption that each person consumes .3 *tael* of salt every day. Owing to the lack of reliable statistics of population, the legal determination of the quantity of salt is entirely arbitrary.[1] The latest report (1911) of the Department of Finance on the quantity of product in recent years gives the following information:

(a) Manchuria. There are eight salt fields in *Feng-tien* Province. The total annual output is 700,000 *shi*, each of which is equal to 600 *catties* in weight. *Hei-lung-kiang* Province, having a salt lake, produces about 7,000,000 *catties* of lake salt.

(b) *Chi-li*. This province has eight salt fields, called *Tsang-lo* or Long weed. They annually produce about 800,000 packages. Each package weighs 450 or 460 *catties*.

(c) *Shan-tung*. Seven salt fields are found in *Shan-tung* Province. Three of them produce 1,068,000 packages every

---

[1] *Cf. infra*, p. 73.

year, each package being equal to 390 *catties*. The quantity of production of the other four fields is unknown, because those fields are not subject to the government regulations.

(d) *Shan-si*. This province has a great salt lake, near which are situated three salt fields which are collectively called *Ho-tung* or River's [1] East. During the last five years, the annual product exceeded 6,000 *ming*. Each *ming* is equal to 120 *yin*, and each *yin* is composed of 250 *catties*. Therefore 6,000 *ming* are equal to (6,000 × 120 × 250) or 180,000,000 *catties*.

(e) *Kiang-su*. In *Kiang-su* Province there are twenty-three salt fields, of which twenty are situated on the south bank of the *Hwai* River, and three, on the north of it. The annual product of the South *Hwai* fields is 508,385 *yin*, each of which contains 600 *catties*, and that of the North *Hwai* fields is 502,540 *yin*, each having 400 *catties*.

(f) *Che-kiang*. The *Che-kiang* salt fields are those situated on the east and the west banks of the *Che-kiang* River. There are thirty-two in all, of which twenty-five are found in the *Che-kiang* Province, and the remainder in the *Kiang-su* Province. The quantity of production is uncertain.

(g) *Fu-kien*. *Fu-kien* Province has thirteen salt fields which turned out 244,000,000 *catties* in 1887. The increase of consumption shows the growth of production, although there is no information about the annual product of the last twenty-five years.

(h) *Kwang-tung*. We find twenty salt fields [2] in this province with an annual product of 1,628,914 packages, each containing 205 *catties*. In recent years two new fields

---

[1] The word "river" means the Yellow River.

[2] In addition to these, *Kwang-tung* has one field for storage only.

have been developed, but the quantity of their products has not yet been ascertained.

(i) *Sze-chuen.* This province has 100,814 salt wells. The annual product of these wells is unknown.

(j) *Yun-nan.* Among the twenty-four salt wells in *Yun-nan* Province, the Black Well and the White Well produce over half of the annual output which is less than 40,000,000 *catties.*

THE LEGAL PRODUCTION OF SALT [1]

Province [2]	Legally fixed number of introductory certificates	Number of *catties* per certificate	Total Number of *catties* produced in the year
Sze-chuen			
Kiang-su . . . . . {	(576,158) (360,000)	(600) (400)	345,688,800 144,000,000
Chi-li	662,497	600	397,498,200
Manchuria	600,000	640	384,000,000
Shan-tung	654,920	320	209,574,400
Kwang-tung	814,509	240	195,482,100
Che-kiang	425,155	400 (average)	170,062,000
Shan-si	635,760	250	158,940,000
Fu-kien	534,414	{ (100) (600)	
Yun-nan [3]			
Kan-su [3]			

Forms of Business Enterprise in Salt Production

The production of salt is an inherited occupation; and the producers, constituting a special class of the society, known as the Stove Men,[4] may be dependent undertakers,

---

[1] This table is prepared on the basis of an official report in 1911 by the Department of Finance.

[2] Mongolia annually consumes about 40,000,000 *catties* of salt.

[3] In *Sze-chuen, Yun-nan* and *Kan-su*, the quantity is not counted by certificates. *Cf. infra*, p. 76.

[4] This name is derived from the process of manufacturing salt with stoves.

small independent enterprisers or merely laborers according to the method by which capital is provided. These methods may be summarized as follows:

(a) The field monopolists.[1] In *Kiang-su, Shan-si* and *Sze-chuen* Provnices, where this type is used, the salt fields together with the necessary equipment are owned by the capitalists, known as the monopolistic field merchants, or, in short, the field monopolists. The relation of the producers, *i. e.,* the Stove Men, to their respective field monopolists are like that of the tenants to their landlords. The Stove Men in this case produce the salt independently, but they are dependent on the field monopolists for a market, the law requiring that the salt be sold only to them. The government, the monopolistic distributors[2] or other purchasers must buy salt from the field monopolists at the fields. Therefore, the producers of this type may be described as dependent undertakers.

(b) The monopolistic distributors. This is a combination of the field monopoly and the monopoly of distribution, or in other words, the monopolistic distributors are at the same time the field monopolists. The monopolistic distributors are related to the producers (Stove Men) in like manner as the field monopolists. But instead of selling the salt at the fields, they distribute it themselves. This type is found in *Che-kiang* Province.

(c) The independent enterprisers. In this case the producers (Stove Men) provide and own the necessary means of production. Their product is directly sold to the monopolistic distributors or other buyers. This type prevails in *Feng-tien, Fu-kien* and *Yun-nan* Provinces.

---

[1] The monopolists in *Sze-chuen* where well salt is produced are called the Well Monopolists. The type of enterprise is the same.

[2] *Cf. infra,* p. 77.

(d) The mixed type. The *Kwang-tung* Province adopts the third type. In recent years, the second type has been introduced to certain places. The third type prevails in *Chi-li* Province, but the producers (Stove Men) may borrow capital from the monopolistic distributors through the mediation of the salt administrators on the condition that their product shall be sold to the creditors. Capital is derived in *Shan-tung* Province from five sources, namely, the Bureau of Transportation in the case of government transportation, the monopolistic distributors as enterprisers, the monopolistic distributors as creditors, the partnerships of the producers and the individual producers. In the first two cases the producers are merely wage-earners, while, in the other cases, they are independent enterprisers.

Consumption of Salt

As we have seen, the supply of salt is legally limited in order to secure profits as public revenues. If the salt is not properly distributed, the consumers in some places would enjoy cheap salt at the expense of the consumers of other places, and the profits from salt would be small. In order to fulfil both the social and the fiscal purposes, a plan known as the division of markets (*Yin Ti*) is devised. According to this plan, the country is divided into a number of salt-consuming territories [1] corresponding to the number of salt-producing provinces.[2] As the salt of each salt-producing province is forbidden to be sold in any salt-consuming territories except that legally assigned as its market. The assignment of salt-consuming territories is determined by the following three conditions: (1) the number of con-

---

[1] Each salt-consuming territory consists of a number of districts under the control of several provinces.

[2] The salt-producing provinces are at the same time parts of the salt-consuming territories, because they have consumers too.

sumers in the territories; (2) the productive power of the salt-producing provinces; and (3) the facilities of communication between the salt-producing provinces and the salt-consuming territories.

The assignment having been made, each district of the salt-consuming territories is expected to demand a certain quantity of salt. To meet the demand, a district may be supplied by several monopolistic distributors or several districts constitute the market of a single monopolistic distributor. The subdivision of markets within a territory is subject to change from time to time to bring it into accord with the amount of invested capital of the different monopolistic distributors. But the subdivision of markets is sometimes not followed in certain salt-consuming territories or parts of the salt-consuming territories which are open to the free competition of the common distributors.

The *Feng-tien* salt is supplied to the three provinces of Manchuria, *viz., Feng-tien, Ki-rin* and *Hei-lung-kiang,* and a part of Mongolia adjacent to them. The consuming territories of the other kinds of salt may be found in Appendix B.

THE TOTAL ANNUAL CONSUMPTION OF SALT AT PRESENT [1]

Kind of Salt	Number of *catties*
Sze-chuen	550,860,000
Kiang-su	489,688,800
Chi-li	397,498,200
Manchuria	384,000,000
Shan-tung	209,574,400
Kwang-tung	195,482,100
Che-kiang	170,062,000
Shan-si	158,940,000
Fu-kien	77,200,000
Yun-nan	51,230,000
Kan-su	2,258,100
Total	2,686,793,600

[1] *Report of the Department of Finance,* 1911. *Cf. supra,* p. 73.

Distribution of Salt

By the phrase " the distribution of salt ", is meant the manner in which salt is bought at the fields and transported to the chief cities of the salt-consuming territories, ready to be sold to the retail traders. Here are three chief methods of distribution.

(1) The private monopoly. According to this method, *Yin Piao,* literally translated " introductory certificates ", are issued by the Department of Finance to confer on the holders the exclusive right to buy salt at certain or all fields in a certain salt-producing province, and to transport the same product to its consuming territory for sale. The sale of product may be carried on by their own shops or by other retailers. This method is further differentiated into two types according as the introductory certificates of a certain salt-producing province are held by a holding partnership which is a combination of several partnerships, or a number of separate partnerships or individuals. When the right of distribution is monopolized by a holding partnership, the subdivision of markets within the consuming territory is arranged by the partnerships, otherwise it is determined according to the number of certificates. These monopolistic distributors, whether they are partnerships or individuals, may hold their privileges so long as they pay their royalties according to the agreements, and fulfil any further requirements laid down by the government.

(2) The public monopoly. In the salt-consuming territory where this method is adopted, the introductory certificates are held by the Bureau of Transportation.[1] The work done by the public salt monopoly may be divided into two types. One type consists of the purchase of salt, its transportation and the retail trade. The other type does not include the retail trade.

---

[1] *Cf. infra,* p. 84.

(3) The competitive trade. Whenever the whole or a part of a certain salt-consuming territory is open to free competition owing to lack of applications for the monopoly, a special certificate called *Piao* is issued to confer the holders with right to buy and sell salt. This method has two characteristics which distinguish it from the private or public monopoly, *viz.*, that any person may apply for one or more certificates and that wherever the method prevails, there is no division of markets.

From the fiscal point of view, the government always tries to adopt the method of private monopoly, if possible, because the monopolistic distributors pay or promise to pay in advance a fixed amount of revenue proportional to the number of introductory certificates issued to them, irrespective of the amount of sale. By this means, the government may raise revenues without the investment of public funds as capital and the assumption of business risk. But sometimes no capitalist applies for the monopoly and sometimes the monopolistic distributors surrender their rights, owing to the presence of one or more of the following conditions which make the monopoly unprofitable:

(A) The decrease of demand for government salt. This may be caused by the heavy burden of taxation, the competition of smuggled salt or economic depression.

(B) The difficulty of land transportation. Where there are no railways the cost of distribution sometimes lessens the monopoly profits.

(C) The situation of some districts near the salt fields. This offers a good opportunity to the smugglers.

(D) The absence of commercial development. Of these four conditions, the first three are met either by the public monopoly or by the competitive trade, while only the public monopoly is resorted to as the remedy of the fourth condition.

The methods of distribution in use at present are given in the following table:

Classification of salt by its producing provinces	Methods of distribution
Feng-tien	Private monopoly / Public monopoly
Chi-li	Private monopoly
Shan-tung	Private monopoly / Competitive trade
Shan-si	Competitive trade / Public monopoly
Kiang-su	Private monopoly / Competitive trade
Che-kiang	Private monopoly
Fu-kien	Competitive trade / Public monopoly
Kwang-tung	Private monopoly
Sze-chuen	Public monopoly / Competitive trade
Yun-nan	Competitive trade

Taxation of Salt

Kuan Tsi, a prime minister of the State of *Tsi*,[1] in the Eastern *Chou* Dynasty, 770-249 B. C., thought that the natural resources of a country should be owned by the state, and created the government monopolies of salt, iron, timber and other minerals as the only source of public revenue, because he disapproved taxation as a means of raising public revenues on the following grounds:[2] (A) because the productive capital of a country would be lessened by taxation; (B) because any kind of private properties subject to taxation would depreciate in value; and (C) because taxation cannot be disguised.

As these monopolies yielded adequate revenues the State of *Tsi* became the richest and most powerful of all the rival states. Consequently, the salt monopoly continues to be one of the most important sources of public revenue. Salt is now taxed in five ways. First, the stove tax is a tax

[1] This state corresponds to the Province of *Shan-tung*.

[2] See *Works of Kuan Tsi*.

on land used for salt production. Secondly, the certificate royalty is a tax on the finished product, justified on the ground that the state is the owner of the raw product (salt water). The royalty is levied according to the number of certificates, each of which represents a certain quantity of finished product. Wherever the imposition of a certificate royalty is not adaptable, a lump-sum royalty is substituted. Thirdly, there are various kinds of receipts such as fees from different sorts of public services, rents of public storehouses and other properties, interest on loans of public money, income from surplus salt, profit from money exchange, fines, *etc., etc.,* which are described by the Department of Finance as miscellaneous revenues. Fourthly, the " dropping to ground " [1] duty is a sort of excise duty levied by a salt-consuming province on the salt of a producing province. Such a duty is imposed on the *Kwang-tung* salt by *Kwang-si,* and on the *Sze-chuen* salt and the *Kiang-su* salt by *Kwei-chow.* This is permitted in order to compensate these two poor provinces which have very few sources of revenue. Finally, there is an additional price for special purposes. The foregoing forms of taxation are considered the regular taxes. They are supplemented by the exaction of provincial governments. For instance, most of the provinces treat salt as any other commodity, and lay a *li-kin* duty [2] on it. Moreover, a compulsory contribution is sometimes paid once and for all by the body of monopolistic distributors in some provinces when the governors are called on to support the imperial government, while, in other provinces, different sorts of special tax are levied for different purposes, *e. g.,* public education, orphan asylums, poor relief, *etc.* The rates of these taxes differ from prov-

---

[1] By the phrase " dropping to ground " is meant the place of consumption.

[2] See *infra,* pp. 103-105.

ince to province. Mr. Chang Chien [1] estimates the real
burden of each *catty* of salt in the following figures:

Classification of Salt by its producing provinces	Composite Rates of the Various Taxes
Kiang-su	over .033 *tael* silver
Kwang-tung	.024 - .025 *tael* silver
Yun-nan	" .033 *tael* silver
Chi-li	.02 " "
Shan-si	.017 - .018 *tael* silver
Sze-chuen	" " " "
Che-kiang	.015 - .016 " "
Shang-tung	" " " "
Fu-kien	under .01 " "
Manchuria	" " " "
Average	.018 *tael* or $.027 silver.

Smuggling of Salt

As we have seen, the distribution of salt is legally re-
stricted, competition is allowed only in *Shen-si*, northwest-
ern *Kan-su* and the frontier districts of North *Chi-li* and
North *Shan-si* where the Mongolian salt is consumed. But
illegal competition is found practically everywhere. Such
is (a) the competition between private salt and government salt; (b) the competition between different salt-producing provinces whose distributors try to sell their salt
beyond their respective consuming territories; and (c) the
competition between different monopolistic distributors in

---

[1] Mr. Chang Chien, now about 70 years of age, is one of China's
most learned scholars as well as one of its greatest practical men.
He never accepted an appointment from the Manchu government.
He devoted his time to industry, commerce, education and various
social activities, and has become the most influential and popular
man in South China. He is a native of *Kiang-su*, the greatest salt-
producing province, and is the greatest living authority on the salt
industry. President Yuen Shi Kai, who holds him in the greatest respect, has appointed him President of the Department of Agriculture,
Industries and Commerce. Mr. Chang has accepted this post.

the same province who try to sell salt beyond their assigned markets. Any competitor other than the monopolist of a certain market is regarded as a smuggler[1] of that market, and his salt, as smuggled goods. Therefore, a smuggler may be a tax-evader or a monopolist, sometimes even government salt being regarded as smuggled goods.

The smugglers take advantage of the following conditions: (1) the contact of markets with one another; (2) the evasion of taxation; (3) the different tax rates in the different provinces; (4) the difference in the cost of production in the different provinces; (5) the difference in the cost of transportation; (6) the pressure of the field monopolists on the producers (Stove Men), *i. e.,* low stove price;[2] (7) the pressure of the monopolistic distributors on the consumers, *i. e.,* high market price;[3] (8) the pressure of the monopolistic distributors on the field monopolists, *i. e.,* low buying price; (9) the secret reduction of tax rates on the part of some administrators in the hope of making up the legal amount of revenue by permitting the producers to make large sales at low rates when difficulty is experienced in selling the proper amounts at the legal rates; (10) the dishonesty of the administrators and detectives; and (11) the inefficiency of the administrators. So long as one or more of these conditions exist, it is impossible for the government to check the smuggling of salt even by inflicting heavy penalties on the smugglers.[4]

---

[1] Any poor person over sixty or under fifteen years old has the right to buy and sell not more than forty *catties* every day without being treated as a smuggler.

[2] *Cf. infra,* pp. 87-88.

[3] *Ibid.*

[4] According to the Penal Code of the *Tsing* Dynasty, no penalty can be inflicted on a person unless the person himself and his salt are both taken as the evidence of smuggling.

Administration of the Salt Monopoly

(1) The administrators. At the beginning of the *Tsing* Dynasty, commissioners were annually appointed by the Emperor to all the salt-producing provinces except *Sze-chuen* and *Yun-nan*. All the administrative officials connected with the salt monopoly were under the direction and supervision of their respective commissioners, leaving those in *Sze-chuen, Yun-nan* and *Kwei-chow* to be controlled by their own governors. Somewhat later it was found that the commissioner in a province was neither so efficient in controling administrative officials nor so familiar with the local conditions as the governor and that it was difficult for the commissioner to discharge his duties satisfactorily. During the period 1660-1860 the governors superseded the commissioners one after another as the supervisors of the salt monopoly. The changes came in 1660 (*Kwang-tung*), 1723 (*Fu-kien*), 1778 (*Shan-si*), 1821 (*Che-kiang, Shen-si, Kan-su*), 1837 (*Kiang-su, Shan-tung*), and 1860 (*Chi-li*). Under the governor is the President of the Salt Department. The latter is the active administrator controling a number of salt administrators and the district magistrates who participate the administration of the salt monopoly. The salt administrators who are specially appointed for this function, consist of two classes, the departmental secretaries and the field (or well) administrators. The departmental secretaries help the president to discharge his duties, while the field administrators enforce the regulations governing the production and sale of salt at the fields and collect all the taxes on salt. In addition to these two classes, the salt departments of a few provinces, like *Kiang-Su,* have one or more vice-presidents and a few inspectors. Each vice-president takes charge of a number of fields in the province and the duty of the inspectors is to see whether the actual quantity of salt

passing by their bureau, situated near the fields, corresponds to the amount of purchase as written in the " bill of drawing salt ".[1] On the other hand, the district magistrates are responsible for the amount of sale assigned to their respective districts, and for the capture of smugglers. As the President of the Executive Department, the circuit governors, the prefects and the superior magistrates are the superior officials of the magistrates, they assume joint responsibility with respect to the duties of the magistrates. It is evident that the governor and practically all of the officials under the Executive Department and the Salt Department of a province are directly or jointly responsible for the administration of the salt monopoly. For a deficit of the legally fixed amount of revenue, they are subject to forfeiture of salary, degradation, removal from office or confiscation of property, the penalty varying according to the amount and term of deferred payment, as well as the direct or joint responsibility which the different ranks of officials assume. Again, the officials may be promoted or recorded for promotion, whenever they are able, by an increase of demand for salt, to secure more than the legally fixed amount of revenue.

(2) The administrative machinery of public monopoly. Whenever the public monopoly of distribution prevails, two types of bureau are especially established, besides the government storehouses. The first is called the Bureau of Transportation, and the second, the Bureau of Wholesale. The bureaus of transportation, of which there may be one or two in a province, are established in a salt-producing province. The bureaus of wholesale are established in the principal cities of the consuming provinces. Both types of bureau generally have a few branches. Candidates for cir-

---

[1] *Cf. infra*, pp. 85-86.

cuit governorships are appointed by the governor of a salt-producing province to be the presidents of these head bureaus, while candidates of district magistrates are appointed presidents of branch bureaus. As their ranks are almost or exactly equal, the presidents of the Salt Department, the Bureau of Transportation and the Bureau of Wholesale are unwilling to be subject to one another. As a result there is no co-operation and the management of public monopoly is generally inefficient. When the Bureau of Wholesale is not required to sell its salt to the merchants, the magistrates are its selling agents. So each magistrate has to carry a certain quantity of salt to his district, and to open a few government salt shops.

(3) The regulation of transportation. In those provinces where the private monopoly of distribution is adopted, two schemes are devised to prevent smuggling. One is to inspect the amount of purchase near the fields, and another, to prescribe the waterways of transportation. For these purposes, " introductory certificates ", " bills of drawing salt " and " waterway tickets " are provided. The introductory certificates issued by the Department of Finance, were formerly brought by the commissioners to the provinces. Since 1748 the governor of each salt-producing province has sent an official to Peking to apply for the required number of certificates for his province. On each certificate the following articles are written:

(a) The certificate represents the quantity of salt thereon stated.

(b) Salt carried with an old certificate is considered as smuggled goods.

(c) Salt carried without the certificate is considered as smuggled goods.

(d) Any one who counterfeits the certificate is put to death.

(e) Any merchant who keeps the certificates over ten days after the sale of salt is beaten forty blows.

(f) The name of an assigned market.

The certificates are distributed among the monopolistic distributors by the President of the Salt Department in a province. Then the distributor may take his certificate (or certificates) to the inspector whose duty it is to clip the certificate at one corner and to hand it to the President of the Salt Department for stamping seal. The latter, then, issues a bill of drawing salt to the distributor. This bill is written that a certain quantity of salt may be bought by Mr. So-and-so at a certain field during a certain period. The quantity of salt bought with this bill must be inspected by an inspector of the Bureau of Inspection near the field. This bill, together with the inspector's report, having been submitted to the President of the Salt Department for approval, is kept in the bureau, while the introductory certificate is returned to the distributor. Whenever the salt is ready to be transported to an assigned market, a waterway ticket is given to the distributor permitting the salt to be carried unmolested from place to place, provided that it is carried by the prescribed waterway and to the destination, as written on the ticket. But the waterway ticket and the introductory certificate are subject to examination by the district magistrates on the voyage, and must be returned to the Salt Department through the magistrate of the consuming district within ten days after the salt has been sold. If either of these documents were not carried with the salt, or any article of the regulations stated on them were violated, the salt would be seized as smuggled salt.

The method of competitive trade may be illustrated by the practice in the North *Hwai* fields of *Kiang-su* Province. In each field there is a government shop, at which any person is allowed to buy salt. When the salt is being carried through the exit of the field, the carrier must pay to the Bureau of Taxation there the required amount of tax on the quantity of salt he has bought. In return for the payment, a certificate stating the carrier's name and native place, the quantity of salt, and the name of the consuming district is given to the carrier. He is allowed to sell the salt in another district with the permission of the magistrate of the district which he first intends to supply. But he is forbidden to sell the salt beyond the territory which adopts the method of competitive trade, and to carry it without the certificate. The certificate must be returned, after the sale, to the Salt Department through the magistrate of the consuming district.

(4) The regulation of price. There are two kinds of legal price, namely, the stove price and the market price.[1] The stove price is the purchasing price from the producers known as the stove men. It is fixed according to the cost of production and the quality of the product. The cost of production in the different provinces depends chiefly on the cost of living of the stove men, and the method of production. Secondly, the market price is the selling price to the retail traders. This is based on the purchasing price, the cost of management and transportation and the taxes. In general, the farther the market is from the salt fields, the more its consumers must pay for the salt. Theoretically, the object of legalizing these prices is to protect, on the one hand, the producers against the field monopolists and the monopolistic distributors and, on the other hand, the consumers against the monopolistic distributors. In practice, however, the terms are favorable to the monopolists. But the regulation has not been renewed since the reign of Emperor Tao

---

[1] The term "market price" is used parallel with "stove price" to indicáte the legal price of salt put in market instead of the economic price determined by the laws of supply and demand.

Kwang, 1821-1850. Therefore, for more than a half-century, the producers and the consumers have been entirely at the mercy of the monopolists.

General Features of the Salt Monopoly

The foregoing discussion should be supplemented by some general considerations. Especially worthy of notice is the relation of the monopoly to the public welfare, the defects of the taxation system, and the present status of the monopoly.

(1) The pressure of the monopolistic distributors upon the actual producers (Stove Men) is of three kinds. The first is that the purchasing price is fixed by the administrators at the expense of the actual producers. Then extra large tubs or baskets are used, when the price is fixed in terms of a tub or basket. The third method is to raise the value of money. Where the fields are monopolized by the field monopolists who are subject to the pressure of the monopolistic distributors too, the actual producers suffer both directly from the field monopolists and indirectly from the monopolistic distributors. The actual producers cannot escape the pressure, because they are compelled by law to continue their pursuit and because they are not acquainted with the agricultural arts or with other pursuits.

(2) The pressure upon the consumers is as great as that upon the actual producers. Take the *Kiang-su* salt for example. As means of transportation are very good within the consuming territory of this salt, the price should be low. On the contrary, the retail price is from sixteen to twenty times the cost of production (the purchasing price from the actual producers). According to Mr. Chang Chien's [1] record which appeared in the *Eastern Times,* Shanghai,

---

[1] *Cf. supra,* p. 81, note 1.

January 4th, 1913, the retail price of this salt is thirty cash [1] in the producing districts; fifty to sixty cash in the farther districts in *Kiang-su* Province; over one hundred cash in *An-hwei* Province; over one hundred and ten cash in *Kiang-si* Province; and over one hundred and twenty cash in *Hu-peh* Province. At first, the pressure falls on the consumers by raising the cost of living. Ultimately, the pressure must also be felt by the landlords and the enterprisers. But as the rise of wages is always slower than the increase of salt price, the laborers suffer the most, though the inevitable effect of dear salt is the retardation of the progress of the whole community.

(3) The treatment of tax-evaders is very unjust. The poor people who smuggle salt are sentenced to imprisonment or death. But the administrators, the monopolists, and the carriers have a right to evade taxation without punishment. For instance, the monopolists of the South *Hwai* fields in *Kiang-su* Province in practice sell over seven hundred *catties* of salt for each six hundred *catty* certificate. In the second place, each vessel or wagon always carries a certain quantity of untaxed salt, known as the " extra salt ". The administrators en route often take a certain quantity of the " extra salt " called the " merit salt " without paying the price.

(4) The salt monopoly is very productive. It yields almost one-fourth of the annual tax revenue.[2] But the possibility of increasing the productivity of the tax is very slight. For, to increase the rate, keeping the production quota at the same figure, would be to induce more smug-

---

[1] The legal rate of exchange is that one thousand cash is equal to one *tael* of silver. But the market rate of exchange fluctuates greatly at different times and places.

[2] According to the budget of 1911, the amount is about 46,312,355 *taels*.

gling. On the other hand, it is impossible to increase the production quota, for the additional salt could not be disposed of because of the competition of the smugglers. The administration of the monopoly is uneconomical; in 1909 and 1910 it consumed about twelve per cent of the average annual return. Further, the tax rates are different in different provinces and at different times; and so this form of taxation is very unjust and uncertain. In the last place, the lack of uniformity in the process of collection and the varieties of supplementary charges in the different provinces make the system very bad. Mr. Chang Chien [1] says, " I cannot see into the complications, though I have investigated these intricate methods of collection for twenty years. But it seems to me that such local practices are not worthy of existence."

(5) The method of large-scale production has never been adopted in any salt-producing province. Everywhere salt is produced by the actual producers (stove men) using primitive methods. The so-called field monopolists are interested only in securing a share of the monopoly profit of the monopolistic distributors and do nothing toward the improvement of production methods. The lack of modern methods is responsible for the high cost of production such as that found particularly in the South *Hwai* fields in *Kiang-su* Province, the bad quality of salt as in *Shan-si, Shen-si* or *Kan-su* Provinces and the decentralization of fields as in *Fu-kien* Province. A still more important effect of the present system is the inability of the government to control the smugglers whose existence strikes at the very heart of the whole system.

(6) The assignment of a particular salt-consuming territory to a particular salt-producing province inevitably raises

---

[1] *Cf. supra*, p. 81, note 1.

two intricate problems. First, the equilibrium of demand and supply of the different salts cannot be preserved. For instance, the salt of the South *Hwai* fields in *Kiang-su* Province has a demand greater than the supply, while there is an oversupply of salt of the North *Hwai* fields in the same province. Assuming the absence of smuggling, the consumers must decrease consumption and pay higher prices in the former case, while the monopolists who look for maximum profits would prefer to waste the surplus products rather than to sell all their products too cheaply in the latter case. In both cases the waste is due to the legal restriction of markets. Fortunately, the problem is solved by the smugglers. In the second place, the demand and supply in particular places cannot be adjusted even under the protection of private monopoly. Two extreme cases may be cited. The protected markets in a territory which is situated far from any salt field, and where the means of transportation is very difficult, have never been supplied by the monopolistic distributors. On the other hand, those markets within a short distance from any salt field are oversupplied due to the competition of smuggled salt. In both cases the government is obliged to take up the work of distribution. Thus the monopolistic distributors are induced to supply only those places which are neither too far from, nor too near to the salt fields, and where the means of transportation are fairly convenient. In a few years the salt fields will be easily accessible to all sections of the country, for the resources of salt are well distributed by nature and railway development is rapidly proceeding. Of course, railway rates will have to be properly adjusted. Under these new economic conditions, the monopolistic distributors will be subjected to severe competition, which they may not be able to survive. But this does not mean that the salt monopoly is doomed. A combined monopoly of both production and distribution might be very successful and might prove to be a highly desirable institution in a transition period in the industrial development of China.

CHAPTER V

Taxation of Commodities

The Regular Customs

(1) General considerations. The customs duty is a general excise tax on merchandise. It finds its origin as far back as the Western *Chou* Dynasty (112-771 B. C.) It was originally levied not for a fiscal, but for a regulative purpose, *viz.*, in order to check the progress of commerce in favor of agriculture. This is because both economists and statesmen at the time thought that agriculture was more fundamental and important than other pursuits. But, at the beginning of the Western *Han* Dynasty (206 B. C.-6 A. D.), it was realized that, in spite of the tax, commerce had progressed. Nevertheless the customs duty was retained, so that, for centuries, the revenue purpose has been primary. At present, custom-houses have been established on the seaboard, on rivers, inland water-ways, land routes and land frontiers. They are called the Regular Customs in order to distinguish them from the Maritime Customs. The jurisdictions of the two systems sometimes seem to conflict. Thus commodities carried by sailing ships are taxed by the Regular Customs, while commodities carried by steamers pay their duties to the Maritime Customs. Formerly, there were thirty-four customs-houses (branches not included) under the control of the Department of Finance. Besides these, a number of customs-houses which was formerly under the control of the Depart-

ment of Public Works has been turned over to the Department of Finance in recent years. At present, there are about twenty-seven important customs-houses as given in the subjoined table.

LOCATION OF CUSTOM HOUSES

Name	Location
Tsung-wen Gate	Peking
Newchwang	Feng-tien Province
Tientsin	Chi-li "
Chin-wang-tao	" "
Kalgan	" "
Che-foo	Shan-tung "
Kiao-chow	" "
Lin-ching	" "
Kwei-hwa-ching	Shan-si "
Sha-fu-kou	" "
Shanghai	Kiang-su "
Hwai-an	" "
Yang-chow	" "
Feng-yang	An-hwei "
Wuhu	" "
Kiukiang	Kiang-si "
Gung	" "
Foo-chow	Fu-kien "
Hang-chow	Che-kiang "
Wen-chow	" "
Han-yang	Hu-peh "
Wu-chang	" "
King-chow	" "
Sun-chow	Hu-nan "
Chungking	Sze-chuen "
Canton	Kwang-tung "
Tai-ping	Kwang-si "

(2) Subjects of taxation. Almost all of the regular customs levy duties on merchandise which is classified into four classes, namely, clothes, food-stuffs, articles of common use and sundry goods. This does not include the taxation, as laid by certain customs, on carts, cattle, brokers,

conveyance of real estate, oil shops, wine shops, salt, bamboo, timber and tea. Most of the customs on the seaboard or on inland waterways also levy port dues (*Chuan Liao*) on junks. At some customs, the following exemptions are made:

(A) In the case of junks.

    (a) Junks carrying government rice or other products.

    (b) Junks carrying rice, bought for famine relief and soldiers' pay (exempt only in *Kiang-su* Province).

    (c) Junks carrying rice or wheat (at certain customs).

    (d) Fishing boats sailing along the sea coast.

    (e) Small boats less than five feet wide.

(B) In the case of goods.

    (a) Copper, lead, tin and other articles bought for government use.

    (b) Rice and other cereals bought for famine relief.

    (c) Rice and other commodities going out of Peking through the *Tsung-wen* Gate.

    (d) Rice or wheat (at certain customs).

    (e) Rice for local consumption, passing by the *Yang-chow* customs, *Kiang-su* Province.

    (f) Pearls and precious metals passing by the *Canton* Customs.

    (g) Food products and other articles necessary for the use of sailors on any vessel.

    (h) Any article borne by a person over his (or her) shoulder or on his (or her) back.

    (i) A certain quantity of native produce of North China, brought southward in the government rice junks.

(j) Tribute from the nobles and lamas of Monoglia, Thibet, *etc.*

(k) Imperial presents to the nobles and lamas of Mongolia, Thibet, *etc.*

(3) Rates and revenues. The rates on both junks and merchandise are specific. In the case of junks, the number of masts, the number of stores or the width of the junks is taken as the basis of rate-making. At a given customs, rates vary not only as the different classes of junks, but also as the different size of the same class. Furthermore, junks of the same class and of uniform size pay different amounts of port dues at different customs. In the case of merchandise the determination of the rate is based on four conditions, namely, the place of production, the degree of utility, its market price, and the distance of transportation. These are taken into consideration for the following reasons: (1) the quality of an article differs with the different places of production; (2) the utility of an article is more or less adapted to the habits of the consumers in different places; and (3) the cost of transportation is directly proportional to the distance.

It is evident that a higher rate should be charged on an article of better quality, more adaptable to the habits of consumers in a certain locality, paying cheaper cost of transportation. With this end in mind, rates are calculated on different units—weight, length, piece, roll, sheet, suit, pair, volume, head, basket, jar, *etc.*—according to the nature of goods subject to taxation. At some customs, a lump sum is levied according to the quantity of goods, measured either by the volume of the junk or by the size of the cart as the case may be. The rates as such are fixed by the Department of Finance and are subject to change from time to time by the department. In addition to the regular duty. a sup-

plementary duty of ten per cent of the regular one is levied
by almost all of the customs under the name of meltage
fee,[1] transportation fee,[2] and others.

The amount of revenues drawn from the different customs is composed of two parts, the regular revenues and
the surplus revenues. Both parts are fixed by law. The
whole of the regular revenues and at least sixty per cent of
the surplus revenues must be paid to the Department of
Finance. It is required that deficits shall be made up by the
administrators out of their private purses as a penalty for
their inefficient administration. But if there is any surplus,
the total sum collected must be sent to the treasury of the
Department of Finance.

(4) Mode of levying duties on goods. The first step
taken by the customs officials in levying duties is to post the
existing rates of dutiable goods on the boards erected at the
markets, and to request the local authorities to print the
same rates in pamphlets for the use of shopkeepers. As
soon as any merchant hands in a report of his goods, the
customs officials must examine the goods and calculate the
amount of duty. The merchant has the right to put the
money into the " collection box " himself without any re-
straint or interference by any customs inspector or watch-
man. One shopkeeper is not allowed to pay tax for others,
except at the *Tsung-wen* Gate of Peking, when the goods
arrive earlier than the owner. In return for his payment,
the merchant is entitled to a red receipt, of which a duplicate
is sent to the Department of Finance for investigation.
This receipt is clipped at its corner, and stamped on its face
with a written time and date of passing, when it is ex-
hibited as the right to pass the customs lines. Duty-paid

---

[1] This fee is charged for the loss of silver in melting.

[2] This fee is charged because the collected revenues must be transported.

goods are allowed to pass twice a day. It is further required that produce from certain localities pay duties at particular customs-houses. For example, any merchant carrying oxen, sheep or goats, camels, horses, or skins overland from *Kiata, Ku-lon, etc.* (Mongolia), to the interior must pay duties at *Chan-tsia-kou* rather than at *Ku-pei-kou.* Secondly, any person carrying goods, along the *Yang-tze* River, from North *Kiang-su* or *An-hwei* Provinces to the City of *Soo-chow* (South *Kiang-su* Province) or the City of *Hang-chow* (Che-kiang Province) must pay duties at the *Wu-siie* Customs,[1] instead of any customs on the seaboard. Thirdly, produce from *Fu-kien, Che-kiang, Feng-tien,* and *Shan-tung* Provinces, transported along the seacoast to Shanghai is taxed by the Shanghai Customs. Fourthly, produce carried from *Fu-kien, Kwang-tung* or *Kiang-si* Provinces to the City of *Soo-chow* or the City of *Sung-kiang* (South *Kiang-su* Province), by the *Che-kiang* River, is taxed at the *Pei-sin* Customs,[1] while that from the latter cities to the former provinces, at the *Che-hai* or the *Pei-sin* Customs. Whenever any attempt to conceal the goods, or to make an incorrect report or to escape payment by taking another route is found, it is treated as an act of evasion. Such an act is punished by a confiscation of half the quantity of goods and a punishment of the merchant according to the civil code, unless the amount of duty evaded is very insignificant (only a few *taels*), when an additional duty of from two to five times the regular duty is imposed as a fine.

(5) The administration of the regular customs.[2] Every customs, together with its branches, is superintended by an official, called the Superintendent of Customs. The superintendent may be

---

[1] *Cf. infra*, p. 99.

[2] Since 1901 many regular customs are under the control of the Inspector General of the Maritime Customs.

(A) An Imperial High Commissioner of Customs, as the Superintendent of the *Tsung-wen* Gate (Peking), that of the Left-Wing (Peking), or that of the Right-Wing (Peking).

(B) A Manchu general, as the Superintendent of the *Foo-chow* Customs.

(C) An Imperial Commissioner of Silk-manufactures, as the Superintendent of the *Si-sin* Customs (*Nan-king*), that of the *Wu-süe* Customs (*Chin-kiang*), or that of the *Pei-sin* Customs (*Hang-chow*).

(D) A Commissioner of Customs, appointed by the Emperor upon the nomination of the Department of Finance, as the Superintendent of the *Hwai-an* Customs (*Hwai-an*),[1] that of the Canton Customs, that of the Tientsin Customs, that of the *Tsau-liang-ting* Customs (*Tung-chow*),[2] that of the *Chang-tsia-kou* Customs (*Kalgan*), or that of the *Sha-fu-kou* Customs (a boundary town between *Shan-si* and Mongolia).

(E) A Circuit governor (or lower local authority), as the superintendents of all the customs, except those mentioned above, and the *Pei-hai* Customs [3] (superintended by the Superintendent of the Canton Customs).

The chief duties discharged by the superintendent are as follows:

(A) To collect the duties mentioned in the preceding section.

(B) To keep an " entry book ", a " collection account " and a " total receipt account ". An entry book is a book in which the merchants enter their goods themselves. A collection account is a record of payments from goods as en-

---

[1] *Hwai-an* is a prefecture in *Kiang-su* Province.

[2] *Tung-chow* is a river port of Peking.

[3] A port on the Canton River.

tered in the entry book. Duplicate copies of the collection account and the total receipt account are kept in the customs and in the superintendent's residence.

(C) To deliver the collected revenues to the Department of Finance once every season (at some customs), or once every half-year (at other customs), or once a year (at still other customs).

(D) To prohibit the trade of the following contraband goods: gambling instruments, salt, tea, opium, saltpetre, cast iron and other munitions of war.

(E) To issue licenses to junks trading along the seacoast or with foreign countries, and to cancel the same upon the return of the junks.

(F) To restrict the exportation of rice, raw silk, satin and cast iron necessary for home use. With respect to rice and cast iron, each junk is allowed to carry an iron pan for cooking rice, an iron axe and a necessary amount of rice corresponding to the number of sailors. Of silk, satin or coarse raw silk, each vessel may carry a certain quantity according to its destination to use in exchange for foreign goods; the exportation of fine raw silk is absolutely prohibited. The maximum quantity to be carried annually by each vessel is as follows: (a) From *Kiang-su* or *Che-kiang* Provinces to Japan, 3,960 *catties* (33 rolls) satin, for 1,200 *catties* or less of which may be substituted coarse raw silk. (b) From *Fu-kien* or *Kwang-tung* Provinces to Annan 300 *catties* coarse raw silk. (c) From *Che-kiang* Province to the Straits Settlements, 2,000 *catties* coarse raw silk. (d) From *Kwang-tung* Province to Sweden, 10.000 *catties* coarse raw silk. (e) From *Fu-kien* Province to any place abroad, 2,000 *catties* coarse raw silk.

(G) To prevent unlawful acts of the inspectors or watchmen.

For these duties, especially the first three, the superintendent is responsible to the Department of Finance. Therefore, the entry books and accounts of every customs must be submitted to the department to be audited once a year. If the superintendent is a commissioner whose term is one year, he must return to the department with the " entry books " and accounts within a fixed period, after the expiration of his term, the time being arranged according to the distance of the customs from Peking. If the superintendent is a local authority, the " entry books " and accounts must be submitted through the governor or governor-general, once a year, although his term is not limited to one year. If the " entry book " or the " red receipt duplicates " are not sent to the department at the right time, the superintendent is fined a half-year's salary. If any merchant is excluded from the right to enter his goods in the " entry books " himself, or to receive a red receipt, the superintendent is fined one year's salary. In the case of a deficit in the revenues the superintendent is punished by a forfeiture of one year's salary, if the deficit is less than five per cent of the legal amount; by degradation to lower and lower rank successively, if over five per cent, ten per cent, twenty per cent, thirty per cent, or forty per cent; and by dismissal if over fifty per cent. To cover the cost of collection he is permitted to retain the supplementary duty or, if a supplementary duty is not levied, to deduct ten per cent out of the surplus revenues.

(6) General features of the regular customs duties. The most interesting feature is the fee system. According to the report of the Investigation Committee sent by the Department of Finance in 1906 to investigate the actual administration of the regular customs, the rates of fees are greater than the rate of the regular duty in all the customs. For example, three or four *taels* of fees are added to every one *tael* of duty in the *Hwai-an* Customs (*Kiang-su* Province),

the *Feng-yang* Customs and the *Wu-hu* Customs (*An-hwei* Province) ; and the amount of fees charged by the *Hwai-an* Customs on timber is ten-fold the amount of duty. As the total sum of fees and duty is sometimes too great to be borne, the corrupt administrators often reduce the regular duty in order to get the sufficient amount of fees for their own account. This necessarily involves five grave defects, namely, unproductiveness 'owing to the secret reduction of duty; various losses due to interference with trade; and injustice, uncertainty and inconvenience because of the discrimination involved in the bargain between the administrators and the merchants. Another corrupt practice is the over-supply of clerks and servants. Each customs has two or three thousands of these persons. They are simply parasites receiving very low wages and trying to take advantage of the merchants. In regard to the regular duty, four points are worthy of mention. First, it should be more productive, as it yields only 6,990,845.925 *taels* according to the budget of 1911. Secondly, it checks the development of internal commerce, because commodities carried by the sailing ships—and most of the internal commerce is conducted in this manner—are subject to the repeated taxation of several successive customs. Goods carried by steamers pay duty to the maritime customs once and for all. Thirdly, the burden on those goods carried by sailing ships is by no means equal. This is due partly to the difference of trade routes and partly to the lack of uniformity regarding to the articles taxed. On the one hand, some goods pass more and the others fewer customs. On the other hand, some customs restrict themselves to a levy of either port dues or customs duties, while the others collect both of them. Further, the taxation of food-stuffs as well as articles of enjoyment and the difference of tax rates and regulations oppress the people with different degrees of severity.

Finally, the pre-determination of the annual return leads to the concealment of revenue. This is done in three ways. One way is to report less than the collected amount in order to save the remainder to remit as part of the deficiency amount required to be paid to the Department of Finance. Another way is to create a sinking fund for a year of deficit. The third is to keep the surplus revenue for provincial purposes, lest the Department of Finance should know the growth of revenue, and increase the fixed amount.

The Li-kin Duty [1]

(1) General considerations. The *Tai-ping* Rebellion broke out in 1850; and from that time one city after another fell into the hands of the rebels. Owing to the fall of *Nanking* and *Soo-chow,* the two most important cities in *Kiang-su* Province, in 1853, the government could not levy the land tax in *Kiang-su,* the most productive of the provinces. The only source of revenue available for military expenses was the customs duties collected by the Imperial Maritime Customs at Shanghai. This drove the authorities to devise new forms of taxation. Mr. Lay Yi Hien, then leading a military force in the Prefecture of *Yang-chow, Kiang-su* Province, introduced the " *li-kin* contribution " with a collection bureau at *Sin-nü Tsin,* a commercial town of *Yang-chow;* and a collection bureau was soon established at Shanghai. The so-called " *li-kin* contribution " is a contribution of one-thousandth of one *tael* of silver charged as a transit duty on the value of goods. The government thought that this compulsory contribution, or duty, would yield a reliable income; and, in 1854, instructed the governor of *Kiang-su* to apply it to the whole

---

[1] The general features of this duty are similar to those of the regular customs duties.

province, if possible. During the period 1854-1874, it was adopted by the eighteen provinces of China Proper, and *Feng-tien* and *Ki-rin* in Manchuria.

(2) Rate and revenue. As we have seen that the *li-kin* duty means a compulsory contribution of one-thousandth of one *tael* of silver, charged as a transit duty on the value of goods, it may be called, in other words, an ad-valorem duty of one-tenth of one per cent. But, in practice, the imperial government has never enforced this legal rate because of the necessity for greater revenue than it produced to defray military expenses during the Rebellion and to carry out local improvements afterward. Rates are different from province to province and from time to time. Nor are they uniform in regard to different classes of goods, which are classified, for taxation purposes, into merchandise in general, salt, tea, opium and other staple produce. According to the *Institutes of the Tsing Dynasty,* the legal rates in the different provinces are one per cent, two per cent, five per cent or nine per cent. But they vary widely in practice. Furthermore, the burden of this tax cannot be measured by the rate alone on a given class of goods, in a given province, at a given time; in addition the number of *li-kin* stations or barriers en route, which varies with place and time, must be taken into consideration.

With respect to revenues, there are no legal amounts to be delivered to the Department of Finance. But this does not exclude it from the right to get a share of revenue by a negotiation with the governors. In order to avoid the great demand and possible interference of the department, the governors keep secret the actual amounts of collected revenues to meet the growing expenditures of their respective provinces. Therefore, the amount of collected revenue reported to the Department of Finance is recognized by almost every well-informed Chinese to be false.

(3) The administration. Since the *li-kin* duty was created for military expenses during the *Tai-ping* Rebellion, it was subject to the absolute control of the governors who were in command of government forces as well as in charge of war revenues. The practice still exists, because the tax has remained after the rebellion as a local rate levied for the purposes of local improvements. For administrative purposes, each province establishes a chief collection bureau at its capital, a number of branch bureaus at the principal cities, and a number of stations. These stations are situated not far apart, along the different trade routes within the province for taxation and inspection purposes. The administrators are selected by the governor from the candidates for circuit governor, prefect, magistrate, *etc*. An administrator is recorded as efficient or inefficient by comparing the amount of collected revenue. He is not allowed to report a less amount than what he has collected, or to report paid-up duty as deferred payment. Whenever he does either of these things, he is punished for fraud on revenue by removing him from office and rank, and by compelling him to make up the deficit, no matter whether the sum is large or small. But he may deduct ten per cent from the collected revenue as the cost of collection.

CONCLUSION

REGARDED from a theoretical standpoint, the Chinese
government is centralized, the several governors being
simply the agents of the Emperor. In fact, however, the
administration is decentralized, because the governors
within their respective provinces are almost independent
in the exercise of their powers. For the sake of efficiency
and economy, the administration of finance naturally falls
in the hands of the governors. As each governor is responsible to the Emperor for his province, he tries his best
to develop its financial productiveness by using all the revenues at his disposal. From the individual point of view,
the governor is loyal to the Emperor. From the national
point of view, however, he can be blamed for the neglect
of his neighbors. In order to prevent such provincial an-
tagonism, the power of financial control is vested in the
legislative departments, especially the Department of Finance. Unfortunately, this check has two undesirable
effects. One of these is the scrambling of revenues. Thus
deficient provincial governments eagerly request the support of the Department of Finance, which, in turn, must
depend entirely upon the aid furnished by the richer provincial governments. Sometimes other departments also
ask for support from the richer provinces. In all cases,
the success in securing additional revenue depends entirely
upon the personal influence of the heads of the different
departments. Secondly. there is a concealment of revenues
which arises from the fact that the governors of the richer
provinces are unwilling to share their revenues with the

Department of Finance. Such concealment is possible because the department is ignorant of the local conditions. Therefore, the department's powers of appropriation and supervision are merely nominal. If we desire to solve the financial problem, we are first confronted with the question of centralizing the administrative powers. But such a question of reorganization will not be solved until the full development of the means of communication.

The development of railways will have an enormous influence upon the tax system. As we have seen, the monopoly in the distribution of salt owes its existence to the difficulty of transportation. Furthermore, the change of trade routes due to the development of railways greatly affects the productivity of the inland regular customs. A new plan of levying the excise tax, better adjusted to the new economic conditions, must soon be devised. Finally, the railways will alter land values, to which the land tax must be adjusted in the future. A general re-assessment will, therefore, be necessary. Thus it is evident that the political organization and the taxation system now in force in China are fit to survive only so long as backward conditions continue. But it must be remembered that such conditions still exist in most sections of China and that they will be slow to disappear. Radical changes will, therefore, come much more slowly than some may expect.

APPENDIX A

THE units of measure and weight of the Chinese system, used in this work, may be expressed in terms of those of the metric system as follows:

One *mou* is equal to $6\frac{144}{1000}$ ares.
One *sinc* is equal to $1\frac{355}{10000}$ litres.
One *catty* is equal to $596\frac{816}{1000}$ grammes.
One *tael* is equal to $37\frac{301}{1000}$ grammes.

APPENDIX B

THE CONSUMING TERRITORY [1] OF THE CHI-LI SALT

Province	Number of prefectures in the province		Number of direct districts in the province		Names and location of the prefectures and direct districts with or without the Chi-li salt	
	Total [2]	With Chi-li salt	Total [2]	With Chi-li salt	Names [3]	Location
Chi-li [4]..	11	9	10	6	Cheng-ta Fu (without)	North of the Great Wall
					Chao-yang Fu (without)	" " "
					Tsi-feng Chow (without)	" " "
					Chang-tsa-kau Ting (without)	" " "
					Tu-shi-kau Ting (without)	" " "
					Ta-lun-nor Ting (without)	" " "
Ho-nan [5]	9	5	5	2	Chang-ta Fu (with)	North of the Yellow River
					Wei-fay Fu (with)	" " "
					Hwai-ching Fu (with)	" " "
					Kai-feng Fu (with)	Eastern Ho-nan
					Chen-chow Fu (with)	" "
					Shü Chow (with)	" "
					Chen Chow (with)	" "

[1] For markets of different salt-producing provinces see *Amendments of the Institutes of the Tsing Dynasty*, chaps. ccxxi-ccxxix.

[2] The total number of prefectures and direct districts in this and the following tables is taken from *Geography of the Chinese Empire* (Shanghai, 1911), by Professor Tu Chi of the Imperial University of Peking.

[3] When the names of places without the *Chi-li salt* are given it is

THE CONSUMING TERRITORY OF THE SHAN-TUNG SALT

Province	Number of prefectures in the province		Number of direct districts in the province		Names and location of the prefectures and direct districts with the Shan-tung salt [1]	
	Total	With Shan-tung salt	Total	With Shan-tung salt	Names [2]	Location
Shan-tung.	10	10	3	3	Shang-tung Province (with)	
Ho-nan...	9	1	5	..	Kwei-ta Fu........ (with)	Northeastern corner of Ho-nan
Kiang-su [3].	8	1	3	..	Shü-chow Fu ...... (with)	Northwestern corner of Kiang-su

understood that the other places are supplied with this salt, **and** *vice versa.*

[4] All places outlying north of the Great Wall are supplied with **the** Mongolian salt.

[5] *Siang-ching,* a subordinate district of *Shü Chow* is not the consumer of the *Chi-li* salt. *Wu-yang,* a subordinate district of *Nan-yang Fu* in southwestern *Ho-nan* is supplied with the *Chi-li* salt.

[1] *Su-chow,* a subordinate district of *Feng-yang Fu,* in *An-hwei* Province is near to *Shü-chow Fu* and supplied with the *Shan-tung* salt.

[2] When the names of places with the *Shan-tung* salt are given, it is understood that the other places are not supplied with this salt.

[3] Three of the eight subordinate districts in *Shü-chow Fu* are not supplied with the *Shan-tung* salt.

THE CONSUMING TERRITORY OF THE SHAN-SI SALT

Province	Number of prefectures in the province		Number of direct districts in the province		Names and location of the prefectures and direct districts with or without the Shan-si salt	
	Total	With Shan-si salt	Total	With Shan-si salt	Names [1]	Location
Shan-si [2]	9	7	10	10	Ta-tung Fu (without)	Surrounded by the Great Wall
					Shau-ping Fu (without)	" "
Shen-si	7	3	5	3	Si-an Fu (with)	Middle part of Shen-si
					Chien Chow (with)	" "
					Pin Chow (with)	" "
					Tung-an Fu (with)	" "
					Shing-an Fu (with)	Southern frontier of Shen-si
					Siang Chow (with)	Southeastern corner of Shen-si
Ho-nan [3]	9	2	5	2	Ho-nan Fu (with)	South of the Yellow River & western part of Ho-nan
					Shen Chow (with)	" "
					Yü Chow (with)	" "
					Nan-yang Fu (with)	" "

[1] When the names of places without the *Shan-si* salt are given, it is understood that the other places are supplied with this salt, and *vice versa.*

[2] According to the *Institutes of the Tsing Dynasty, Ta-tung Fu* and *Shau-ping Fu* are markets of the *Shan-si* salt.

[3] *Siang-ching,* a subordinate district of *Shü Chow* in *Ho-nan* Province is supplied with the *Shan-si salt. Cf. supra,* p. 110, note 5.

THE CONSUMING TERRITORY OF THE SHEN-SI OR KAN-SU SALT

Province	Number of prefectures in the province		Number of direct districts in the province		Names and location of the prefectures and direct districts, with the Shen-si or Kan-su salt	
	Total	With Shen-si or Kan-su salt	Total	With Shen-si or Kan-su salt	Names [1]	Location
Shen-si [2]	7	2 (Shen-si) 1 (Kan-su)	5	1 (Shen-si)	Han-chung Fu. (Shen-si)	Southwestern corner of Shen-si
					Yen-an Fu .... (Shen-si)	Middle section of northern corner of Shen-si
					Lu Chow...... (Shen-si)	Northern corner of Shen-si
					Fung-tsiang Fu. (Kan-su)	Western corner of Shen-si
Kan-su [3]	8	5 (Kan-su)	6	2 (Kan-su)	Ping-liang Fu*. (Kan-su)	Eastern corner of Kan-su
					Ching-Yang Fu* (Kan-su)	" "
					Ning-sha Fu*.. (Kan-su)	Northern corner of Kan-su
					Lan-chow Fu‡. (Kan-su)	Northwestern part of the interior of Kan-su
					Gung-chang Fu‡ (Kan-su)	Southern part of Kan-su
					Chin Chow † .. (Kan-su)	" "
					Tsia Chow † ... (Kan-su)	Southern corner of Kan-su

[1] Those places in *Shen-si* and *Kan-su*, whose names are not given here are supplied with the Mongolian salt.

[2] The *Shen-si* salt is derived from the Large Piebald-Horse Lake in *Ting-bien Hsien*, a subordinate district of *Yen-an Fu*. *Ching-tsien Hsien*, a district northeast of *Yen-an Fu* also takes the *Shen-si* salt.

[3] There are two kinds of salt in *Kan-su*, one being lake salt from the Small Piebald-Horse Lake in *Ling-chow*, a subordinate district of *Ning-sha Fu*, another being well salt from salt wells in *Chang Hsien* (now a part of *Lung-si Hsien*) and *Si-ho Hsien*, which are subordinate districts of *Gung-chang Fu*. Those places marked with (*) are supplied with lake salt, while the others indicated by (†), with well salt.

THE CONSUMING TERRITORY OF THE KIANG-SU SALT

Province	Number of prefectures in the province		Number of direct districts in the province		Names and location of the prefectures with or without the Kiang-su salt	
	Total	With Kiang-su salt	Total	With Kiang-su salt	Names [1]	Location
Kiang-su [2]	8	4	3	2	Kiang-ning Fu (with)	Southwestern Kiang-su
					Hwai-an Fu (with)	North of the Yang-tze River
					Yang-chow Fu (with)	" "
					Tung Chow (with)	" "
					Hai Chow (with)	" "
					Shü-chow Fu (with)	" "
An-hwei ..	8	7	5	4	Hwei-chow Fu (without)	Southeastern frontier of An-hwei
					Kwang-ta Chow (without)	Eastern frontier of An-hwei
Hu-peh [3]..	10	9	1	1	Sze-nan Fu (without)	Southwestern corner of Hu-peh
Hu-nan ...	9	9	4	2	Pin Chow (without)	Southeastern frontier of Hu-nan
					Kwei-yang Chow (without)	" "
Kiang-si ..	13	10	1		Kwang-sin Fu (without)	Northeastern corner of Kiang-si
					Nan-an Fu (without)	Southern Kiang-si
					Gung-chow Fu (without)	" "
					Ning-tu Chow (without)	" "
Ho-nan ...	9	9	5	1	Yü-ning Fu (with)	Southern frontier of Ho-nan
					Kwang Chow (with)	Southeastern corner of Ho-nan
Kwei-chow.	12	4	1		Tung-yin Fu (with)	Eastern frontier of Kwei-chow
					Sze-chow Fu (with)	" "
					Chin-yuen Fu (with)	" "
					Li-ping Fu (with)	" "

[1] When the names of places with the *Kiang-au* salt are given, it is

The Consuming Territory of the Che-kiang Salt

Province	Number of prefectures in the province		Number of direct districts in the province		Names and locations of the prefectures and direct districts with the Che-kiang salt	
	Total	With Che-kiang salt	Total	With Che-kiang salt	Names	Location
Che-kiang.	11	11	....	....	Che-kiang Province	
Kiang-su ..	8	4	3	1	Soo-chow Fu.	South of the Yang-tze River
					Sung-kiang Fu . . .	" "
					Shiang-chow Fu...	" "
					Chin-kiang Fu....	" "
					Tai-chwang Chow.	" "
An-hwei ..	8	1	5	1	Hwei-chow Fu . ..	South corner of An-hwei
					Kwang-ta Chow ..	East corner of An-hwei
Kiang-si ..	13	1	1		Kwang-sin Fu....	Northeastern corner of Kiang-si

understood that the other places are not the markets of this salt, and *vice versa.*

[2] *Shü-chow Fu* represents only three of its subordinate districts, namely, *Pi-chow, Su-chien* and *Tsui-ning. Cf. supra,* p. 110, note 3.

[3] *Hoc-feng chow* and *Chang-lau-hsien,* two districts near to *Sze-nan Fu* are not the *Kiang-su* salt markets.

THE CONSUMING TERRITORY OF THE SZE-CHUEN SALT

Province	Number of prefectures in the province		Number of direct districts in the province		Names and location of the prefectures and direct districts with or without the Sze-chuen salt	
	Total	With Sze-chuen salt	Total	With Sze-chuen salt	Names [1]	Location
Sze-chuen .	12	12	8	8	Sze-chuen Province (with)	
Hu-peh [2] ..	10	1	1		Sze-nan Fu (with)	Southwestern corner of Hu-peh
Yun-nan [3] .	14	2	3		Tung-chuen Fu (with)	Northeastern corner of Yun-nan
					Chao-tung Fu (with)	" "
Kwei-chow	12	8	1	1	Tung-yin Fu (without)	Eastern frontier of Kwei-chow
					Sze-chow Fu (without)	" "
					Chin-yuen Fu (without)	" "
					Li-pingFu (without)	" "

[1] When the names of places with the *Sze-chuen* salt are given, it is understood that the other places have not this salt, and *vice versa*.

[2] *Hoc-feng-chow* and *Chang-lau-hsien*, two districts near to *Sze-nan Fu* are also supplied with the *Sze-chuen* salt.

[3] *Tsien-yih-chow, Nan-ning-hsien* and *Ping-yi-hsien*, three districts south of *Tung-chuen Fu* are also supplied with the *Sze-chuen* salt.

The Consuming Territory of the Kwang-tung Salt

Province	Number of prefectures in the province		Number of direct districts in the province		Names and location of prefectures and direct districts with the Kwang-tung salt	
	Total	With Kwang-tung salt	Total	With Kwang-tung salt	Names [1]	Location
Kwang-tung.	9	9	7	7	Kwang-tung Province	
Kwang-si ...	11	11	2	2	Kwang-si Province	
Kiang-si	13	2	1	1	Nan-an Fu	Southern Kiang-si
					Gung-chow Fu ..	" "
					Ning-tu Chow ...	" "
Fu-kien	9	1	2	....	Ting-chow Fu....	Western frontier of Fu-kien
Hu-nan	9	....	4	2	Pin Chow	Southeastern frontier of Hu-nan
					Kwei-yang Chow	" "
Yun-nan	14	2	3	....	Kwang-nan Fu ..	Southeastern corner of Yun-nan
					Kai-hwa Fu......	" "

[1] *Ku-chow-ting*, a subordinate district of *Li-ping Fu*, eastern frontier of *Kwei-chow* Province is also supplied with *Kwang-tung* salt.

The Consuming Territory of the Fu-kien or Yun-nan Salt

Province	Number of prefectures in the province		Number of direct districts in the province		Names and location of prefectures and direct districts without the Fu-kien or Yun-nan salt	
	Total	With Fu-kien or Yun-nan salt	Total	With Fu-kien or Yun-nan salt	Names	Location
Fu-kien.	9	8 (Fu-kien)	2	2 (Fu-kien)	Ting-chow Fu † (Fu-kien)	Western frontier of Fu-kien
Yun-nan	14	10 (Yun-nan)	3	3 (Yun-nan)	Kwang-nan Fu † (Yun-nan)	Southeastern corner of Yun-nan
					Kai-hwa Fu † (Yun-nan)	"　　"
					Tung-chuen Fu * (Yun-nan)	Northeastern corner of Yun-nan
					Chao-tung Fu * (Yun-nan)	"　　"

¹ Those prefectures marked with (†) are the *Kwang-tung* salt markets. Those indicated by (*), together with three neighbor districts, are supplied with the *Sze-chuen* salt. *Cf. supra*, p. 115, note 3.

A LIST OF SELECTED REFERENCES IN CHINESE

Institutes of the Tsing Dynasty (Shanghai; 5th ed., 1909)—Called, in
Chinese, *Ta Tsing Hui Tien* and edited by a board of editors appointed by the government.

Amendments of the Institutes of the Tsing Dynasty (Shanghai; 5th
ed., 1909)—Called, in Chinese, *Ta Tsing Hui Tien Shih Li* and
edited by a board of editors appointed by the government.

Inquiry into the Institutions of China (Shanghai, several editions)—
The most complete history of institutions of the different dynasties,
being called, in Chinese, *Wên Hsien Tung Kao* or *San Tung Kao*.

Essays on the Institutions of the Tsing Dynasty (Shanghai, 1901)—
Comprises a number of essays written by Mr. Wang Ching-Yun,
sometime president of the Department of Public Works. This
work is called, in Chinese, *Shi Chao Tsi Tseng*.

Works of Kuan Tsi (Shanghai, several editions)—Published as a
special treatise or as a part of the works of Chinese philosophers.

Governmental System of the Chou Dynasty, 1122-249 B. C. (Shanghai)
—Serves as a model of the governmental system in the different
dynasties, being called, in Chinese, *Chou Kuan* or *Chou Li*.

Memorials in the Reign of Emperor Kwang Shü, 1875-1908.

Memorials in the Reign of Emperor Shüan Tung, 1909-1911.

DATE DUE

DEC 17

GAYLORD

PRINTED IN U.S.A.